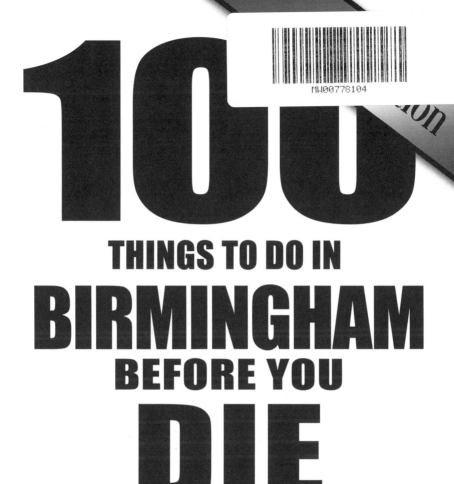

100

THINGS TO DO IN

BIRMINGHAM

BEFORE YOU

DIE

Birmingham Civil Rights Institute Dome

100
THINGS TO DO IN
BIRMINGHAM
BEFORE YOU
DIE

2nd Edition

Enjoy the magic!

Verna Gates

• •

VERNA GATES

REEDY PRESS

Copyright © 2022 by Reedy Press, LLC
Reedy Press
PO Box 5131
St. Louis, MO 63139, USA
www.reedypress.com

Library of Congress Control Number: 2021952871

ISBN: 9781681063751

Design by Jill Halpin

All photos by the author unless otherwise noted.

Printed in the United States of America
22 23 24 25 26   5 4 3 2 1

DEDICATION

To the city of my birth and my heart. Your iron mountains
always pull me back, like a magnet to my soul.

Alabama Theater

CONTENTS

Preface xiii

Acknowledgments xv

Food and Drink

1. Pass the James Beard Awards at Highlands Bar and Grill 2

2. Heat Up at One of the Hottest Restaurants, Hot and Hot Fish Club 4

3. Make It Automatic for Seafood 6

4. Get a Taste of the Gulf at the Fish Market 7

5. Red Light Means Go to Chez Lulu 8

6. Coddle Your Egg at Satterfield's 9

7. You'll Be Over the Moon at the Bright Star 10

8. Join a Family Affair at Gianmarco's 11

9. Ride the Blimp to Roots and Revelry 12

10. Yo' Mama Knows Her Fried Chicken 13

11. Carve Steaks That Hang off the Plate at Lloyd's Restaurant 14

12. Soar with Soul Food from the Heart at Eagle's Restaurant 15

13. Indulge in a Vegetarian's Dream at a Steak and Seafood Restaurant 16

14. Brake for Lunch at the Original Whistle Stop Café 17

15. No Need to Go to Philly for a Great Cheesesteak 18

• •

16. Comfort Food Found a New Comfort Zone at Johnny's Restaurant 19

17. A Lot of Shaking Going On at Green Valley Drugs 20

18. Pop Goes the Summer Heat with Popsicles and Ice Cream 21

19. You Won't Find Your Average Junkyard Dog at Gus's........................... 22

20. Milo's Is Known for Its Hamburger, Famous for Its Tea 24

21. Black-Eyed Peas and Turnip Greens Make Pizza Southern Style 26

22. Pit Masters Rule in Alabama Barbecue... 28

Music and Entertainment

23. Soar as High Culture Dances, Sings, and Plays 34

24. Drink in an Opera Shot.. 35

25. LOL in Real Time at the Comedy Club 36

26. Periodically, You Need a Drink at the Collins Bar 37

27. Unfold a Jazzed-Up Paper Doll 38

28. Bow Before the Queen.. 39

29. Rise as the Moon Shines on the Sleeping Lady 40

30. Blast Off to Saturn—Out of This World 41

31. Park Yourself in the Garage for a Great Time.. 42

32. Steel Away to Iron City... 43

33. Remember Mom's Basement?.. 44

34. Kiss the Marble Ring 45

35. Join the Quest for an Alternative 46

● ●

36. Feel Foxy at the Fennec 47

37. Take the Brews Cruise, It's Pretty Crafty 48

38. Find the Best Music and Dancing, Bar None 50

39. At 2 a.m., Where Do You Go? To the Nick 51

40. Make Moorish Fun at the Alabama Theater 52

41. Return to the Golden Era at the Lyric Theater 53

42. Encounter Reel Fun at the Sidewalk Film Fest 54

43. Tune to Colonial with the National Sacred Harp Singing Convention... 55

44. Salute Birmingham for Starting Veterans Day Parades 56

45. Going to the Dogs on Do Dah Day 57

46. Make the Magic City Art Connection, Bridging People to Art 58

47. Shhhh . . . Find the Secret Stages 59

48. Party with Gusto at the Greek Festival 60

49. Embrace Your Inner Tacky at the Wacky Tacky Light Tours 61

Sports and Recreation

50. Accelerate to Talladega Superspeedway 64

51. Get Your Motor Running at Barber Motorsports 65

52. Play Ball at Regions Field/Classic at Rickwood 66

53. Be Bullish on Birmingham 67

54. Walk Where Legends Live On 68

55. Honor the Greats at the Negro Southern League Museum 70

56. Feast on Football, Food, and Fun at the Magic City Classic 71

57. Tee Off at Robert Trent Jones Golf Courses 72

58. Set Your Compass for Oak Mountain State Park 73

59. Canoe the Cahaba, Swim in a Swimming Hole 74

60. Get Rolling at Railroad Park 76

61. Trunks Are Up at Avondale Park 77

62. Spring for Snowflakes in Aldridge Gardens 78

63. Follow the Iron Road at Red Mountain Park 79

64. Learn a Boulder Way to Live at Moss Rock Preserve 80

65. Have a Blooming Good Time at the Birmingham Botanical Gardens ... 81

66. Horn In on a Roaring Good Time at the Birmingham Zoo 82

67. Amp the Amphibians at the Salamander Festival 83

Culture and History

68. Vulcan, the God of the Forge, Watches over Us 86

69. Experiment at the McWane Science Center 87

70. Dig the Time before Dinosaurs Roamed 88

71. Enter Birmingham's Antebellum Past at Arlington 89

72. Meet the Spirits Who Haunt Us 90

73. Hear Stories Come Alive at Oak Hill Cemetery 91

74. Picture Centuries of Beauty at the Birmingham Museum of Art 92

75. Prepare for a Sensory Overload at Joe Minter's Yard 93

● ●

76. Trace the Road to Freedom on the Civil Rights Trail 94

77. Have a Blast at Sloss Furnaces 96

78. Take Off at the Southern Museum of Flight 97

79. Feel Young Again at the Samuel Ullman Museum.................................. 98

80. No Tuxedo Required at the Alabama Jazz Hall of Fame 99

81. Watch Perfection Made Perfect at Virginia Samford Theatre................ 100

82. Grasp the Edge of Your Seat at Birmingham Festival Theatre............... 101

83. Put a Song in Your Heart at Red Mountain Theatre 102

84. Act Right for the Children 103

Shopping and Fashion

85. Local Is Great at Alabama Goods 106

86. Sip the Spirits of the First Lady of Liquor 107

87. Seek Southern-Style Glam at Gus Mayer.................................. 108

88. Flash Fashion-Forward at Etc 109

89. Get Back to the basic 110

90. Go Where Comfort Is in Style 111

91. Put the Man Back in Men's Fashions 112

92. Step Back into Old-World Elegance at Shaia's of Homewood 114

93. Sprinkle Your World with Fairy Dust and White Flowers..................... 115

94. Get Dolled Up for Barbie's Dreamhouse 116

95. Take the Dr. Pepper Cure 117

• •

96. Every Book Is Signed at the Alabama Booksmith 118

97. Purchase the Past on the Alabama Antique Trail 120

98. Shop a City Store Older than the City, Bromberg's 122

99. Get Your Peanuts at the Peanut Depot 123

100. Reed Books and Museum of Fond Memories 124

Activities by Season 127

Suggested Itineraries 130

Index 139

• •

PREFACE

It was called the Magic City—a bright, shiny, new boomtown following the misery of the Civil War. Birmingham was teething on steel as a brash Wild West town with gambling, shootouts, and famous madams. When the steel died down, banking and medical industries settled it into a sophisticated city with a famed culinary scene, multiple entertainment districts, and striking natural beauty. The colorful past remains in a renovated vaudeville theater, a haunted cemetery, and mining sites transforming into a greenway connecting the city from east to west. The city changed the country with its notorious struggle, preserved in churches, parks, and the Birmingham Civil Rights Institute. The city is experiencing a new boom with the bustling historic downtown, craft beer scene, nationally recognized chefs, and an explosion of music venues. The Magic is back.

● ●

View of Birmingham from Red Mountain

ACKNOWLEDGMENTS

Thank you, Mark Peavy, for your incredible photos of a city and its people that we both love. Thank you, Annette Thompson, for giving me such a great start on this book.

• •

Chez Fonfon server and Frank Sitt (right)

FOOD AND DRINK

PASS THE
JAMES BEARD AWARDS
AT HIGHLANDS BAR AND GRILL

When 28-year-old Frank Stitt wanted to open a European-based gourmet restaurant in Birmingham, bankers did not feel hungry. Turning to family and friends for funding, the aspiring chef opened Highlands Bar and Grill in 1982 as an innovator in the burgeoning farm-to-table movement. His foresight was rewarded in 2018, when Highlands brought home the Best Pastry Chef award and was named the Most Outstanding Restaurant in America by the James Beard Foundation. Today, he owns four restaurants: Highlands, the Italian-based Bottega Restaurant and Bottega Café, and a casual French bistro, Chez Fonfon. Locals know to arrive early on Thursdays at Highlands and Fonfon to savor the crab cakes. Other favorites include baked grits at Highlands, desserts at Chez Fonfon, and Parmesan soufflé at Bottega. The favorite cocktail, the "orange thing," was created quite by accident, but the delightfully refreshing martini successfully battles Alabama heat. City leaders often gather for a drink at Highlands Bar.

2011 11th Ave. S
highlandsbarandgrill.com, fonfonbham.com

Bottega
2240 Highland Ave.
bottegarestaurant.com

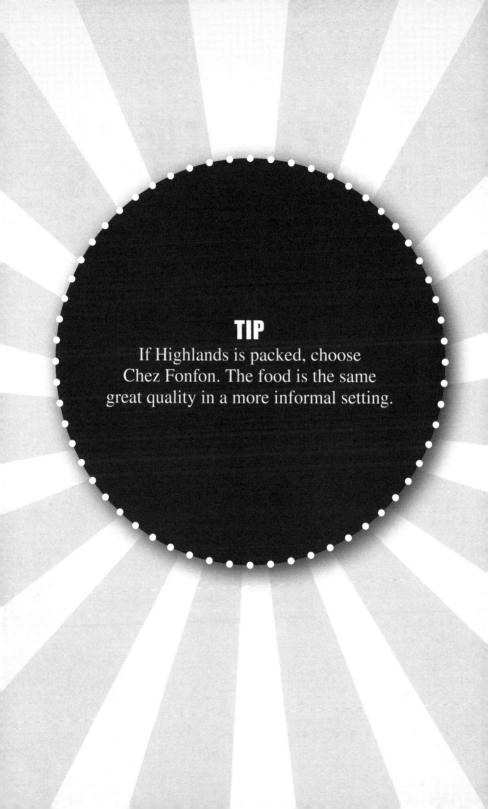

TIP

If Highlands is packed, choose
Chez Fonfon. The food is the same
great quality in a more informal setting.

HEAT UP AT ONE OF THE HOTTEST RESTAURANTS,
HOT AND HOT FISH CLUB

When tomatoes come into season, the word goes out for the beloved Hot and Hot Tomato Salad listed on the 100 Dishes to Eat in Alabama Before You Die app, along with the pickled okra. The chef/owner of Hot and Hot Fish Club and Ovenbird, Chris Hastings, has captured James Beard awards, and also defeated Bobby Flay on *Iron Chef America*, with a dish now served as his Iron Chef Ravioli. Hot and Hot blends French, California, and Southern cooking styles plus local farmers' produce into a unique flavor. Ovenbird opens into a garden with its open-door and open-fire-concept restaurant. The small-plate menu offers delicacies ranging from a Beef Fat Candle to Octopus Salad. The live-fire grilling theme originated in Spanish and Southern traditions. A local beer company created a signature brew for Ovenbird to complement its craft cocktails.

2901 2nd Ave. S, Ste. 110, 205-933-5474
hotandhotfishclub.com

2810 3rd Ave. S, 205-957-6686
ovenbirdrestaurant.com

TIP
Start at the bar with a small plate
at Ovenbird and switch over to
Hot and Hot Fish Club for your meal.

MAKE IT AUTOMATIC
FOR SEAFOOD

Fresh Gulf Coast oysters from boutique seafood farmers stand in varying degrees of rawness, ready to be savored by the waiting taste buds of diners. Automatic Seafood and Oysters was founded by an Alabama native, Chef Adam Evans and his wife, Suzanne. While building an acclaimed reputation in Atlanta, he was wooed back home by the enticing restaurant renaissance in Birmingham. Don't be surprised if you find Alabama white sauce brought down from his Muscle Shoals roots. He mixes it with a crispy fish collar dotted with chili butter and subtle fish ribs. Pair your flaky fish with a bold cocktail and experience the flavor pop Evans provides with his pairings. Located in the Lakeview Entertainment district, the historic building opens up to outdoor seating, where live music can be heard from nearby clubs.

2824 5th Ave. S, 205-580-1600
automaticseafood.com

GET A TASTE OF THE GULF
AT THE FISH MARKET

George Sarris barely set a toe in his new American home before he found a kitchen. Arriving from Greece in 1969, he joined the Greek restaurant dynasty by washing dishes the next day at Niki's, owned by his uncles. He opened a fish market to sell Gulf shrimp and seafood, which soon morphed into the Fish Market Restaurant and Oyster House, which puts a Greek twist on Alabama fish. His famed Athenian-style fish comes topped with grilled onions, marinated Greek olives, sliced tomatoes, creamy feta cheese, and Greek spices. George's oyster stew features plump oysters in a rich base so filling it is best eaten as an entrée. Whether Greek style or low-country po'boy, everything comes with Southern-style sides: collards, black-eyed peas, and fried okra.

612 22nd St. S, 205-322-3330
thefishmarket.net

TIP
Order the blue crab claws. This is a small, native crab with a sweet, flavor-packed taste. You will pay more for the same crab at upscale restaurants.

RED LIGHT MEANS GO
TO CHEZ LULU

With rich, warm, red walls, crushed velvet pillows, and velvet paintings, Chez Lulu makes a tongue-in-cheek reference to French "Madame Lulus"—code for red-light districts. Add sidewalk seating and Chez Lulu captures the best of French café society. The food, featuring soups, tartes, pizza, and a long list of delectable desserts, is inspired by the authentic European breads baked in the adjoining Continental Bakery, which is where the café idea began. Some come to Lulu just for the Lulu cheese with fresh bread or the salad sampler. While the restaurant may teasingly recall a bordello, the bakery operates as a serious medieval shop, with old-world handcrafted skill and natural ingredients going into every baguette. The art of food is occasionally accompanied by an accordion, dancers, opera singers, jugglers, Brazilian drum corps, or Moroccan gypsy fiddlers.

1911 Cahaba Rd., 205-870-7011
chezlulu.us

TIP
The breads from the Continental Bakery are delicious. Dip away in the savory oils.

CODDLE YOUR EGG
AT SATTERFIELD'S

As a stay-at-home mom, Becky Satterfield grew organic vegetables and watched Julia Child. She never suspected the two hobbies would collide into one of Birmingham's best restaurants. Satterfield's Restaurant "grew organically," much like the meat and produce she so carefully selects for her often French-based recipes. Her popular coddled egg appetizer is classic Satterfield: caramelized onion, carrots, and celery doused with cream and cheese, with the pierced yolk of a poached egg—comfort food supreme. Take a Southern standard, such as pork chops and a sweet potato, add a bacon-stuffed chili relleno on a bed of apple mole, and the result is the highly recommended Duroc pork chop. Top it off with beignets with sautéed apples and homemade vanilla bean ice cream.

3161 Cahaba Heights Rd., Vestavia Hills, 205-969-9690
satterfieldsrestaurant.com

YOU'LL BE
OVER THE MOON
AT THE BRIGHT STAR

An itinerant artist needed a few good meals as he traveled through the South. The long-forgotten artist left behind classical murals in this restaurant, which has passed its 100th birthday. The Bright Star Restaurant began as a horseshoe-shaped cafe bar founded by a Greek immigrant. Today, it seats 330 and is operated by the same family. In 2010, the James Beard Foundation named it an American Classic, a lifetime achievement. What hasn't changed is the Greek-style snapper and steaks, the fried snapper throats, and the homemade seafood gumbo. The 100 Dishes to Eat in Alabama Before You Die app lists the broiled seafood platter as a fish-lover's dream with Gulf red snapper, shrimp, oysters, and scallops, finished off with lobster and crab meat au gratin. The homemade pies tower with whipped meringue. At lunch, you can indulge in a meat-and-three (vegetables) menu.

304 19th St. N, Bessemer, 205-426-1861
thebrightstar.com

JOIN A FAMILY AFFAIR
AT GIANMARCO'S

In the beginning, Birmingham attracted large numbers of Italian immigrants, setting a high bar for great Italian food. Gianmarco's Restaurant raised that bar. Owned by an Italian father and two sons, its family pride in cuisine breaks out into fettuccine, linguine, rigatoni, and lasagna that are always served hot. The waiters line up at the open kitchen, waiting for the steaming plates that spend just moments on the counter. One of the sons, Marco, prefers old-world comfort food. When regulars get a whiff of Marco making his braciola, the non-reservation tables at the bar fill up fast. Brother Giani prefers modern fusion for creative nightly specials. Father Giovanni, the "pretty face" out front, greets guests with his charming Italian accent. The whole family turns out to hand-make the pasta from custom Italian pasta flour.

721 Broadway St., Homewood, 205-871-9622
gianmarcosbhm.com

RIDE THE BLIMP
TO ROOTS AND REVELRY

When your restaurant sits below the world's only remaining zeppelin mooring tower, your menu has to fly high. Roots and Revelry Restaurant walks the line between the roaring-'20s glam of the old Thomas Jefferson Hotel and the hip new JT Tower. The menu reflects not its white tablecloth, but white marble tabletops. The menu is packed with great fine-dining offerings: braised lamb shank, duck leg quarter, and wild Atlantic salmon. The cocktail menu nods to Southern roots: mama's sweet tea, haint blue, dove shoot, and garden party. Finish it off with blackberry cobbler. In good weather, sit outside and enjoy the view of the city. Maybe that blimp will finally land.

1623 2nd Ave. N, 205-730-1907
roots-revelry.com

YO' MAMA
KNOWS HER FRIED CHICKEN ...

And her fried fish and fried shrimp and fries. The tea is sweet and the wings are hot. For the gluten-free fried food fan, Yo' Mama's cooks up crispy meats, fish, and fries without the flour. The food is freshly made, just as though your own mother cooked it. A mother/daughter team founded this popular downtown breakfast and lunch spot. Shrimp tacos, grilled or fried, sit on salsa fresca and slaw. Most dishes can be covered in homemade POE sauce— Put on Everything. Chicken and waffles, along with cheese grits, dominate the breakfast menu. Those grits can also be paired with the shrimp. Burgers are covered with a sweet/tangy BBQ sauce from a family recipe. Look out for their special Meal-of-the-Day. It's easy to order online for pickup.

2328 2nd Ave. N, 205-957-6545
yomamasrestaurant.com

CARVE STEAKS THAT HANG OFF THE PLATE
AT LLOYD'S RESTAURANT

For decades, Lloyd's Restaurant denoted the end of civilization, as far as Birmingham travelers were concerned. It stood as a lonely beacon on old Highway 280, as the last stop before the forest took over. Today, development surrounds Lloyd's, one of the oldest restaurants in town. New shops may crowd the down-home restaurant, but they can't cover the sumptuous scent of onion rings emanating from every corner since 1937. Pair those rings with a hamburger steak and you will be eating the meal that draws regulars back for more. The steaks are so big, they hang off the plate, especially the 20-ounce Porterhouse. The full menu includes seafood and barbecue, and the onion rings are listed on the 100 Dishes to Eat in Alabama Before You Die app.

5301 US 280, Hoover, 205-991-5530
lloyds280.com

SOAR WITH SOUL FOOD FROM THE HEART
AT EAGLE'S RESTAURANT

Soul food originated from parts considered unsuitable for fancy tastes, but African American cooks turned pig's ears into the silk purses of flavor. Andrew Zimmern of the Food Network noted the visible bristles along the ear's rim as a sign of genuine soul food in Birmingham's premier soul food spot, Eagle's Restaurant. The family cooks the fatty pig's feet, eking out every nuance of tastiness. For the pork neck bones, they cut and wash each one by hand, then slow-cook it until it melts into its own gravy. The two most expensive menu items come from the humblest ingredients: the chitterlings (intestines) and the oxtail. Please do not attempt cutlery on the tender tail, their most famous dish, or you are in danger of being branded a Yankee. It is properly devoured using the fingers.

2610 16th St. N, 205-320-0099
eaglesrestaurant.com

INDULGE IN A VEGETARIAN'S DREAM
AT A STEAK AND SEAFOOD RESTAURANT

More than 70 items line the long steam table at Niki's West Steak and Seafood Restaurant. The line moves fast, so try to decide early! The cafeteria line is stocked as a classic Southern "meat and three" (meat and three vegetables), with flavorful dishes that nod to the owners' Greek heritage. The good news for vegetarians is that all their veggies are cooked without traditional pork or chicken stock, even the collard and turnip greens. Favorites include the Greek chicken, the lemon pepper catfish, and chocolate meringue pie. For those who prefer a table option, you can order a classic breakfast or a seafood and steak dinner. From the famous stuffed grouper to Greek-style shellfish and fish, the seafood menu items taste as fresh as the water they were swimming in that morning. Come prepared for generous portions and homemade desserts. One clue to remember: banana pudding and cobbler are listed as sides.

233 Finley Ave., 205-252-8163
nikiswest.com

BRAKE FOR LUNCH
AT THE ORIGINAL WHISTLE STOP CAFÉ

Fannie Flagg grew up eating at her great-aunt's restaurant, where fried green tomatoes were a popular item at the "stand" right in front of the small-town whistle-stop. Miss Bess Fortenberry, a single lady with a zest for life, recruited two other lady friends from her work during World War II to join her in the small, but popular, Irondale Cafe. Thus began the *Fried Green Tomatoes at the Whistle Stop Café* of book and movie fame. The original still serves 600 to 800 of the crispy fried delicacies every day. Green tomatoes are firmer than their riper cousins and thrive in hot oil, which seals their plump, fleshy texture and rich flavor. Bess's original recipe remains intact, and the café offers prepackaged boxes with the proper spices for cooking them.

1906 1st Ave. N, Irondale, 205-956-5258
irondalecafe.com

TIP
Come back for the Whistle Stop Festival in late September. Be sure to hear the train riding past the café, and visit the craft and food vendors.

NO NEED TO GO TO PHILLY
FOR A GREAT CHEESESTEAK

Comedian Craig Ferguson visited Salem's Diner and raved about the Philly cheesesteak on his *Late Late Show*. He vigorously defended his proclamation of the best of its kind on the show, fending off doubters. At the small, friendly diner, Wayne Salem reigns over the breakfast and lunch menus. He rarely forgets a customer or his famed father, Ed Salem, one of the 50 greatest members of the Crimson Tide, which has dominated college football for decades. The décor consists of football photos and memorabilia, so if your favorite team has been defeated at the hands of the Tide, focus on the great food. For breakfast, try the dish called the trashcan, a mix of hash browns, spicy sausage, onions, peppers, tomatoes, and cheese.

2913 18th St. S, Homewood, 205-877-8797
salemsdiner.com

COMFORT FOOD FOUND A NEW COMFORT ZONE
AT JOHNNY'S RESTAURANT

While you expect to see white-tablecloth restaurants in the "Oscars of Food," the James Beard awards, it is rare for an old-school, meat-and-three chef to get a nomination. Tim Hontzas, a member of one of Birmingham's restaurant dynasties, refers to his food as a meat-and-Greek. Along with crispy fried chicken and a greens duo of collards and turnip, you will find charbroiled chicken souvlaki or keftedes (Greek meatballs). Hontzas's blackboard lists the menu and gives credit to his epicurean heroes—the local farmers who treat their animals with respect and their veggies with nothing at all. Hontzas insists that farmers hand-grade the picked okra heading for his frying pan. He delights in cooking up happiness or, as the blackboard suggests, "make cornbread, not war."

2902 18th St. S, Ste. 200, Homewood, 205-802-2711
johnnyshomewood.com

A LOT OF
SHAKING GOING ON
AT GREEN VALLEY DRUGS

Take your seat at the historic lunch counter, or slide into a booth at Green Valley Drugs. For more than 60 years, hamburgers have sizzled on the grill along with crisp bacon for an added crunch. Or slather pimento cheese on top of the burger for the recommended medicine for hunger. The old-fashioned milkshakes stick to the basics: vanilla, chocolate, strawberry, and cherry. A homespun shake cannot be mastered with a straw; a spoon is required. The menu offers chili two ways: either canned or homemade; you can expect this level of honesty from the menu and the staff, adding even more character to the experience. Breakfast follows tradition with eggs, grits, bacon, and toast. For the biggest dose of nostalgia, check out the throwback prices.

1915 Hoover Ct., Hoover, 205-822-1151

POP GOES THE SUMMER HEAT
WITH POPSICLES AND ICE CREAM

The poached pear sorbet is poached in red wine at Big Spoon Creamery. Other offerings in this artisan ice cream shop include oatmeal 'scream pie, chocolate orange pistachio, and Meyer lemon meringue pie. Steel City Pops staffers appear at gatherings with their cart, pulling out their Buttermilk Popsicle, which combines a complex duo of flavors: vanilla and cheesecake. Strawberry Lemonade wins the popularity contest. Try the Maple Bacon with Bourbon, the Cucumber Lime, or Sweet Tea. Urban Pops puts out the regulars, but adds Asian and Indian flavors to their sticks. These treats incorporate ingredients from roses to saffron to cardamom. Kulfi, a frozen dairy dessert from India, deepens the flavor into a richer, creamier ice cream.

Big Spoon Creamery
4000 3rd Ave. S, 205-703-4712
927 Oxmoor Rd., Homewood, 205- 637-0823
bigspooncreamery.com

Steel City Pops
2821 Central Ave., Ste. 109, Homewood 205-803-6502
steelcitypops.com

Urban Pops
2760 John Hawkins Pkwy., Ste. 100, Hoover 205-518-0270
urban pops.business.site

YOU WON'T FIND YOUR AVERAGE JUNKYARD DOG
AT GUS'S

Gus Alexander opened Gus's Hot Dogs in the late 1940s, and deposited the tiny shop with the big sauce with Greek cousins when he sailed for home. The grilled dog, with mustard, onions and the requisite secret sauce, was named one of America's 75 best by the Daily Meal website. All day long, you can get breakfast sandwiches made of Alabama's own Conecuh sausages. Not far away, Pete Graphos stirred up his own secret sauce and launched Sneaky Pete's. The claim for this growing dog empire is the famed Sneaky Pete Hot Sauce. His recipe mixes a beef-pork combo and contributes kraut and/or chili, bacon, and either cheese or beef sauce. Beware the "junkyard dog," the fully-loaded-with-everything howler of a dog.

Gus's Hot Dogs
1915 4th Ave. N, 205-251-4540

Sneaky Pete's
sneakypetes.com

TIP
If you want a café experience at Sneaky Pete's, go to the 6th Avenue South shop. Or, take out the dog at one of the gas station stores.

SNEAKY PETE'S LOCATIONS

1101 4th Ave. N, 205-518-6055

3507 6th Ave. S, 205-254-9762

70 Green Springs Hwy., Homewood, 205-945-1519

240 Oxmoor Cir., #107, 205-942-7294

1804 Crestwood Blvd., Irondale, 205-956-6503

5036 Ford Pkwy., Bessemer, 205-426-6080

3229 Hwy. 52, Pelham, 205-621-6448

1550-C Montgomery Hwy., Hoover, 205-979-9482

7200 Gadsden Hwy., Trussville, 205-661-0294

MILO'S IS KNOWN FOR ITS HAMBURGER,
FAMOUS FOR ITS TEA

Many people have tried to guess the secret ingredient in the famed Milo's Sweet Tea, but makers insist the treasured elixir contains only tea and sugar. Its devotees buy gallons of this, the original energy drink. Equally secret since its 1946 founding is the sauce generously poured over a grilled hamburger patty, smothering onions and pickles. A fresh, warm bun tops the Milo's Original Burger. For breakfast, the mini-cinnamon buns hide behind their own discreet recipe. Both the burger and tea are listed in the 100 Dishes to Eat in Alabama Before You Die app. You can only get the burger at one of the many Milo's locations, but the sweet tea can be found in most food and convenience stores.

MILO'S LOCATIONS

1530 Montclair Rd., 205-951-2889

1210 Inverness Corners, 205-991-6456

3965 Crosshaven Dr., Vestavia Hills, 205-637-3535

1449 Montgomery Hwy., Vestavia Hills, 205-823-6456

208 State Farm Pkwy., Homewood, 205-945-8008

5887 Trussville Crossings Pkwy., Trussville, 205-661-2100

209 Gadsden Hwy., 205-833-6363

2020 Pelham Pkwy., Pelham, 205-402-0722

BLACK-EYED PEAS AND TURNIP GREENS
MAKE PIZZA SOUTHERN STYLE

Pepperoni may be the soul food of Italy, but Slice cuts a Southern path with the soul pie: Conecuh sausage, black-eyed peas, turnip greens, bacon, onions, and cheese on a razor-thin crust. With a nod to the nearby Gulf, there's an oyster Rockefeller as well. Wash it back with a cold, local beer from their extensive bar. Post Office Pies made Thrillist's Top 33 Pizza Shops in America for its swine pie, a cardiac-risking, delicious lode of pepperoni, sausage, bacon, cheese, and a bit of basil. Davenport's Pizza Palace cracked the pizza market in the meat-and-three town in 1964 by hand-delivering pizzas to neighbors to introduce "foreign food." The crust is thin and comes cut into squares with your choice of toppings. Chicago-style pizza fans choose Tortugas Homemade Pizza. The deep-dish stuffed pizza is on the 100 Dishes to Eat in Alabama Before You Die app.

PIT MASTERS RULE
IN ALABAMA BARBECUE

Several noted champions of the pit fire are smoking pork throughout the Birmingham area. Jim 'N Nick's Bar-B-Q Restaurant cooks up their own heritage pigs, grown by Alabama farmers. The cheese biscuits hit the spot and the 100 Dishes app. Full Moon Bar-B-Que is famous for half-moon cookies and marinated coleslaw; both made the 100 Dishes app. The Golden Rule Bar-B-Q and Grill started as a roadhouse in 1891, making it the oldest continuously running restaurant in Alabama. For breakfast, Demetri's hides its barbecue in a giant omelet, a manly meal earning it the number-one spot in *Playboy*'s Best Breakfast in America listing. The Pork-Stuffed Tater may be on the 100 Dishes app for highly awarded Saw's BBQ, but the Pork and Greens say soul-food-delicious. Go to the original Saw's in Avondale. You know a state takes its barbecue seriously when white sauce is considered controversial. Miss Myra has ignored the naysayers for years, while diners line up to eat her crispy and moist chicken dipped in her pale sauce. Bob Sykes Bar-B-Q of Bessemer has dished up its 100 Dishes Pork Sandwich since 1957. Catch the ribs at Rib-It-Up downtown. For Memphis-style, choose Rusty's Bar-B-Q in Leeds.

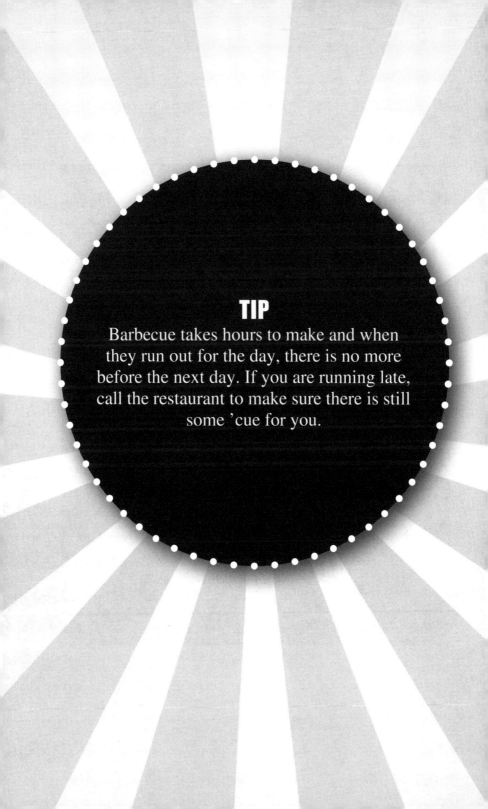

TIP

Barbecue takes hours to make and when they run out for the day, there is no more before the next day. If you are running late, call the restaurant to make sure there is still some 'cue for you.

Jim 'N Nick's Bar-B-Q
1908 11th Ave. S, 205-320-1060
220 Oxmoor Rd., Homewood, 205-942-3336
1810 Montgomery Hwy., Hoover, 205-733-1300
1660 Gadsden Hwy., Trussville, 205-661-3100
jimnnicks.com

Full Moon Bar-B-Que
525 25th St. S, 205-324-1007
337 Valley Ave., 205-945-9997
5988 Chalkville Rd. N, 205-655-1515
2000 Patton Chapel Rd., Hoover, 205-822-6666
fullmoonbbq.com

Saw's BBQ
215 41st St. S, 205-591-1409
1154 11th Ave. S, 205-224-4408
1008 Oxmoor Rd., Homewood, 205-879-1937
sawsbbq.com

Golden Rule Bar-B-Q and Grill
2504 Crestwood Blvd., Irondale, 205-956-2678
goldenrulebbq.com

Bob Sykes Bar-B-Q
1724 9th Ave. N, Bessemer, 205-426-1400
bobsykes.com

Demetri's BBQ
1901 28th Ave. S, Homewood, 205-871-1581
demetrisbbq.com

Miss Myra's Pit Bar-B-Q
278 Cahaba Heights Rd., Vestavia Hills, 205-967-6004

Rib-It-Up
830 1st Ave. N, 205-328-7427
ribitup.com

Rusty's Bar-B-Q
7484 Parkway Dr., Leeds, 205-699-4766
rustysbarbq.com

Opera Birmingham

MUSIC
AND ENTERTAINMENT

SOAR
AS HIGH CULTURE
DANCES, SINGS, AND PLAYS

Birmingham ranks as one of the few cities of its size to field high-quality symphony, ballet, and opera companies. The Alabama Symphony Orchestra pushes the boundaries with award-winning, artistically innovative, new American music. With 54 salaried musicians and an internationally acclaimed music director, the symphony performs 190 times per year. The orchestra also sponsors a large Symphony Choir, which performs with them regularly. During the Christmas season they perform Handel's *Messiah*, a beloved holiday tradition. Occasionally, they play for performances of the Alabama Ballet, a nationally recognized company. The Alabama Ballet celebrates the holidays as one of only eight companies in the world permitted to perform *Balanchine's Nutcracker®*. Outside of the classics, they have performed dances such as Blue Suede Shoes, a tribute to the music of Elvis Presley.

Alabama Symphony Orchestra
alabamasymphony.org

Alabama Ballet
alabamaballet.org

DRINK IN
AN OPERA SHOT

If you hear opera in a bar, it's not the whiskey singing. It's Opera Birmingham! This progressive opera company may sing out anywhere in town: at a brewery, in a parking lot, or on a downtown street. All of the Opera Shots are free. Opera Birmingham steps out of the box, putting on new and controversial operas addressing issues such as prisoners of war, unknown soldiers, and civil rights. Children's operas, such as *The Three Little Pigs*, are performed in an outdoor amphitheater in a local park. Traditional operas round out the season. Opera Birmingham annually hosts a vocal competition where young national contenders launch careers. The company recruits national talent for their performances, and takes local vocal artists to the community.

operabirmingham.org

LOL IN REAL TIME
AT THE COMEDY CLUB

The great blizzard of 1993 might have been able to destroy the stage, but it could not stop the laughter. The Comedy Club StarDome survived and thrived and now calls itself the number-one comedy club in the country. From Positively Funny Improv to Open Mic Night, the StarDome features and nurtures local talent. National talent, from James Gregory to Colin Jost to NeNe Leakes and Henry Cho, regularly appears under the StarDome. At the new Star Bar, you can cozy up to your funny favorites as the entertainers join in the fun. There is hope for the humorously challenged. This family-owned club wants to tickle the Magic City and offers classes to whip up your wit.

1818 Data Dr., Hoover, 205-444-0008
stardome.com

PERIODICALLY, YOU NEED A DRINK

AT THE COLLINS BAR

If you are a local, you can play the "Birmingham game" and try to recognize the names and places that replace chemical elements on the Periodic Table behind the bar. Some are obvious, such as the Cahaba River, while others are more obscure: for example, Merrilee, who formerly owned a renowned indie bar. If you flew in, you can enjoy the paper airplane décor. The art on the walls detail the steps for a perfect fold for these flying semi-wonders. As you contemplate the walls and ceiling, don't forget that the Collins Bar's true fame comes from its superb mixologists. The conversation starts with "What do you like?" and the bartender takes it from there. With a backdrop of fine whiskeys, vodkas, Scotch, and bourbons, matched with fresh fruit purees, ginger beers, spices, and a bit of magic, the cocktails refresh and intoxicate the taste buds. Pair it with upscale comfort food.

2125 2nd Ave. N, 205-323-7995
thecollinsbar.com

UNFOLD
A JAZZED-UP PAPER DOLL

Named for a tune penned by jazz vocalists, the Mills Brothers, Paper Doll Bar reflects the Jazz Age in art deco-feel glam. Local art frames the walls and covers the furniture with original designs. Custom cocktails pair with the sophisticated atmosphere to complete an elegant experience. A sense of humor still sneaks in, with drinks with names such as "Thank You for Smoking"—crafted with homemade bacon bitters, proving once and for all that everything tastes better with bacon. Many of the cocktails are conjured from unique brands mixed with flavors from spices, botanicals, and local favorites such as Buffalo Rock Ginger Ale. Snacks go beyond the usual cheese to encompass champagne gummy bears and chocolate espresso beans.

2320 1st Ave. N, 205-201-5005
paperdollbar.com

BOW BEFORE
THE QUEEN

Truly the queen of bartending, Queen's Park Cocktail Bar is co-owned by the first woman to take first place in the Diageo World Class US 2018 bartending competition. Laura Newman then proceeded to take second place in the global competition in Berlin. To say you can get a great drink in this classic cocktail bar certainly classifies as an understatement. Named for the Queen's Park Swizzle crafted in the original Queen's Park Hotel in Trinidad, the bar celebrates the grand hotel era of cocktails. Don't look for the common concoctions here—they celebrate the lesser-known alcoholic beverages by making precise, consistent drinks that will dazzle the drinker. Don't look for food here—just spirits.

112 24th St. N
queensparkbham.com

RISE AS THE MOON SHINES
ON THE SLEEPING LADY

Looking out into the city at night, the moon shines above but never awakens the curious lady's face in the quarter moon. The Classical Revival-style building, dating to 1908, has been reinvented as the Elyton Hotel. It stands in what was called the heaviest corner on earth, weighted with early skyscrapers. The hotel is named for a town that predates Birmingham. Enter to see the marble staircase, rich with striking and colorful veins. Brush past the colorful strokes of local artist Susan Oliver. When you reach the 16th floor, Moon Shine opens up with drinks and views of the city. Be sure to pay homage to the lady sculpted into the curved stone. While there, enjoy crafted cocktails and food from the wood-fired oven.

1928 1st Ave. N, 205-731-3600
elytonhotel.com

BLAST OFF TO SATURN—
OUT OF THIS WORLD

He might be Brian Teasley or Birdstuff from Man or Astro Man? band fame, but he is definitely the founder of Saturn, an otherworldly music venue. Saturn, with a namesake rocket running through it, orbits outer space in the hip Avondale entertainment district. The space-themed club celebrates local jazz great Sun Ra, who claimed Saturn as a spiritual home, and the space race launched in Huntsville. The venue hosts experimental music, causes, trivia nights, and punk rock flea markets. Not all who come to play bring a guitar; you can pick your game from hundreds of selections, from Candy Land to vintage pinball and video games. The Satellite Bar provides two kinds of grains: beer and alcohol and the only all-you-can-eat cereal bar. In the morning, enjoy its coffee shop.

200 41st St. S, 205-703-9545
saturnbirmingham.com

TIP
Occasionally Man or Astro Man? will perform here and just seeing the eclectic audience, some in costume, is as entertaining as the music.

PARK YOURSELF IN THE GARAGE
FOR A GREAT TIME

In the early days of the automobile, chauffeurs sat by the phone in the garage, awaiting a call from wealthy Highland Avenue families. In 1970, the neglected nooks designed for Model Ts were converted into stalls for small businesses, one of them a café. Soon, the café expanded, growing into one of the 10 Bars Worth Flying For in the world, according to *GQ* magazine. An eclectic courtyard with scattered antiques, from pedestal sinks to sculpted cupids, the Garage sets the scene for great conversation, live music, and a cast of characters among the regulars (check out who is occupying the "asshole" seat at the bar). *Esquire* and other magazines have rated it as one of the best bars in America. The top time to stop in is when the wisteria vines bloom.

2304 10th Ter. S, 205-322-3220

TIP
Lunch is a great time to go. The sandwiches are fresh and tasty.

STEEL AWAY
TO IRON CITY

A 1929 car dealership store shifted gears into one of Birmingham's most popular music venues. Iron City rocks with three concert stages, two bars, and a restaurant. The renovators kept the flavor of the light industrial site with metal accents, polished wood and stone, and earthbound colors. It books local, regional, and national bands for its 1,300-person concert hall. On some nights, they show classic movies, such as sci-fi extravaganzas. For some events, for example, when a comedian is booked, tables and chairs are set up for the performance. The secret to maximum comfort for many acts is to reserve a table in the mezzanine. The food and drinks equal the quality of the entertainment.

513 22nd St. S, 205-202-5483
ironcitybham.com

REMEMBER
MOM'S BASEMENT?

Remember the place where all of the teens gathered to play foosball and sneak a beer? It's back! Mom's Basement is a retro dive bar, and yes, it's in the basement of a strip mall. You can revisit all the things you remember, including Mom's picture—patrons are encouraged to bring pictures of their matriarch to hang on the walls. Laid out like a basement entertainment room, it features a pool table, darts, and addictive vintage pinball machines. The throwback décor includes cheap wood paneling, the requisite floral couch, and neon signs. Welcome back to the 1980s—so authentic you will be hunting for eight-track tapes. Make new memories with your buddies inside the old photo booth for a classic, black-and-white strip of goofy grins. Unlike Mom, the bar provides plenty of libations.

4411 3rd Ave. S, 205-774-6667
momsbham.com

KISS
THE MARBLE RING

Enter the Tardis (the blue police phone booth from *Doctor Who*), dial the number, and be welcomed into the speakeasy world. Stuffed chairs and sofas in purple crushed velvet, a giant chandelier, and wallpaper that on closer examination reveals risqué figures combine for 1920s glam. You are tempted to look around for Jay Gatsby. The first flapper, Alabama's Zelda Fitzgerald, inspired the room, the name, and the signature cocktails, each one highlighting her life. The obscure reference cursing someone to "die in the marble ring" is lost in Zelda's oft macabre expressions but suits the neo-Golden Age bar. The gem is hidden upstairs, which you must climb to gain entry.

430 41st St. S, 205-202-3967
marbleringavondale.com

JOIN THE QUEST
FOR AN ALTERNATIVE

It's the nightclub that never closes. You can dance the night, the morning, and the afternoon away. And no one cares who your dance partner may be. The Quest is open 24 hours a day, 365 days per year. The music pumps from DJ shows and karaoke singing. The stage presents male reviews and drag shows, often with midnight start times. The club has served the LGBTQ community for more than two decades. While the club specializes in alternative lifestyles, a mix of straight and gay partiers can be found any time of the day or night. The bar menu reflects this with tongue-in-cheek drink titles: Froot Loop, Sex on the Beach, and Alien Brain Hemorrhage.

416 21st St. S, 205-251-4313
quest-club.com

FEEL FOXY
AT THE FENNEC

The Fennec fox is a nocturnal party animal and the inspiration for this restaurant/nightclub with a honky-tonk feel. More than half of the music is country, with acts such as a Johnny Cash tribute band. The dance floor is big enough to boot-scoot, two-step or line dance, whichever the music demands of your feet. Enjoy a dinner with a rambler's ribeye or a pan-roasted gulf fish. If you are too late for dinner, try late-night bar food such as Conecuh corndogs, nachos, chili cheese fries, or the hitch knot, but not unless you are with your favorite partner. The venue offers local and regional performers such as singer-songwriters and crossover artists. Cocktails naturally include the Foxy Lady, as well as a slurricane.

1630 2nd Ave. S, 659-208-2480
thefennecbham.com

TAKE THE BREWS CRUISE,
IT'S PRETTY CRAFTY

When Avondale Brewing Company opened in an old brothel in a down-and-out neighborhood, it was soon brewing up success— for the 'hood, and for craft beer. Avondale was built on beer, but thrived on events, setting up outdoor music and food trucks. They fired up a new entertainment district by drawing people in. They were soon followed by new craftsmasters: Cahaba Brewing Company, Trim Tab, Good People, and Ghost Train Brewing Company. These brewers launched Birmingham into the fastest-growing craft beer metro area in the US. Back Forty Beer Company upped the game by offering gourmet pub foods. Ferus focuses on sour brews and burgers as it holds down the Trussville Entertainment District. Jazz plays at True Story Brewing on Wednesday nights. Each brewery offers its own beer, style, and personality.

Avondale Brewing Company
201 41st St. S, 205-777-5456
avondalebrewing.com

Back Forty Beer Company
3201 1st Ave. N, 205-407-8025
backfortybeer.com

Cahaba Brewing Company
4500 5th Ave. S, 205-578-2616
cahababrewing.com

Ferus Artisan Ales
101 Beech St., Ste. 111, Trussville, 205-508-3001
ferusales.com

Ghost Train Brewing Company
2616 3rd Ave. S, 205-201-5817
ghosttrainbrewing.com

Good People Brewing Company
114 14th St. S, 205-286-2337
goodpeoplebrewing.com

Trim Tab Brewing Company
2721 5th Ave. S, 205-703-0536
trimtabbrewing.com

True Story Brewing Company
5510 Crestwood Blvd., 205-593-4144
facebook.com/truestorybrewing

FIND THE BEST
MUSIC AND DANCING, BAR NONE

Live bands play Thursday through Friday, and sometimes on Wednesday, when the Magic City Boppers are on the dance floor. Bar 31 hosts a great house band that plays rock and roll geared towards foot-tapping and body-swaying. A variety of ages turn up for the music and atmosphere. During the day, it's the Soul Food Kitchen drawing in the local crowd. Meat-and-threes (vegetables) satisfy the tummy from 11 a.m. to 3 p.m. It's one of the few places you can get fried chicken gizzards and Rolling Stones cover songs. In the evenings, something is always going on—from bingo to DJs to costume nights. Whether you're dancing, listening to the band or playing a game, Bar 31 provides a place for fun to happen.

1485 Montgomery Hwy., Vestavia, 205-824-3160
bar31bham.com

AT 2 A.M., WHERE DO YOU GO?
TO THE NICK

Billed as "Birmingham's dirty little secret," this scruffy nightclub starts and ends late. It is the last to close: 4 a.m. on Thursday, 6 a.m. on the weekend. Known for the hottest music and coldest beer, the Nick has managed to stay hip for decades. On a given weekend, you may find a local favorite or a regional or national band screaming music past the pirate skull above the bar. They don't play favorites with genres. You could hear blues to bluegrass, rock to rockabilly, punk to pop, or hip-hop to rap. The music starts at 10 p.m. Even though the outside looks as if it is held up by music posters, the Nick is here to stay.

2514 10th Ave. S, 205-252-3831
thenickrocks.com

MAKE MOORISH FUN
AT THE ALABAMA THEATER

A Byzantine prince would feel quite at home in the Alabama Theater, dubbed the Showplace of the South. Its Moorish design exudes a magical charm necessary for a theater built as a Paramount movie palace. It is a place where dreams dance across the big screen and lovers kiss under exotic moons. Today, the big screen reveals the true scope of such classics as the original *Phantom of the Opera* or *Casablanca*. Built for silent movies, the Mighty Wurlitzer Organ rises from beneath the stage before every movie for a sing-along with the audience. Ironically, the rare organ saved the building, as organ enthusiasts raised the preservation funds. Rock concerts, operas, ballets, comedians, and other events fill the stage for the 2,500 seats throughout the year. A Christmas movie series is a favorite holiday activity.

817 3rd Ave. N, 205-252-2262
alabamatheatre.com

RETURN TO THE GOLDEN ERA
AT THE LYRIC THEATER

The Lyric once again rings with laughter and good times. The Marx Brothers, Mae West, Will Rogers, Sophie Tucker, and Milton Berle all walked the boards of the stage of this 1914 theater. Lovingly restored to the glory of its heyday, it shines as one of the few remaining examples of vaudeville theater—designed to bring the audience as close as possible to see and hear their favorite acts. Today, the Lyric stays booked up with bands, dancers, authors, comedians, and storytellers. The broad stage and intimate setting allow the performing arts to engage the audience. With the arching gold stage, the blue-and-gold box seats, and the mural above the stage, the sheer beauty of the Lyric sprinkles fairy dust on every performance.

1800 3rd Ave. N, 205-252-2262
lyricbham.com

ENCOUNTER REEL FUN
AT THE SIDEWALK FILM FEST

Film fans screen the newest documentaries, films, shorts, music, and animated films in some of the oldest venues. The Sidewalk Film Festival inhabits the historic theater district for six days in late August and throughout the year, showing a wide variety of films to a diverse audience. Both the Carver Theater and the Alabama were built with big screens for maximum viewing pleasure. A new theater under the Pizitz Food Hall hosts the year-round showings. Low-priced weekend passes urge attendees to take chances on challenging productions they might not otherwise see. The fresh, engaged audiences attract filmmakers from Alabama and beyond. Generally, the filmmakers attend the screening, providing commentary and answering audience questions. Running concurrently is SHOUT, the state's only film festival focusing on the lives, issues, and artists in the LGBTQ community.

2nd Ave. N, B1, 205-324-0888
sidewalkfest.com

TUNE TO COLONIAL
WITH THE NATIONAL SACRED HARP SINGING CONVENTION

Alabama is ground zero for Sacred Harp Singing. This 300-plus-year-old choral tradition began in colonial America in singing schools teaching young people how to sight-read music. And the National Sacred Harp Singing Convention is held here every June. Sometimes called shape note singing, the hymnals use four distinct shapes of notes to indicate the sound. Uniquely democratic, the a cappella singing style places the singers in a hollow square with four vocal ranges facing each other, making an astonishing sound. Anyone can lead a song. The leader just enters the square, calls out a hymn number, and sings the first verse without words but using the fa-so-la sounds. The sacred harp refers to the voice—the one musical instrument everyone possesses. Anyone attending the singing is welcome to join the choir. People come from all over the world to hear old Alabama families sing the tradition, carried on in small rural churches for generations.

fasola.org

SALUTE BIRMINGHAM
FOR STARTING
VETERANS DAY PARADES

At the end of World War II, a Birmingham veteran decided that Armistice Day, created to honor World War I soldiers, left out the newly returning soldiers, sailors, and airmen. Raymond Weeks gathered a delegation and created a proposal to present to President Dwight Eisenhower. He wanted to include all who have ever served in our military. In 1954, Eisenhower agreed and Veterans Day was born. Weeks led the first Veterans Day Parade in 1947 and every one thereafter until his death in 1985. The grand tradition continues with a new generation of men and women who walk the streets of Birmingham past cheering crowds in one of the largest veterans' parades in the country.

nationalveteransday.org

TIP
Line up along First Avenue to enjoy the parade center. Bring your flags to wave!

GOING TO THE DOGS
ON DO DAH DAY

Has your dog ever expressed interest in wearing a pink tutu? Perhaps camo? Or maybe being a Jedi knight? Do Dah Day truly goes to the dogs in this outrageous pet parade. Be sure to dress sharp—a doggie king and queen are crowned based on $1 votes. People decorate themselves, their cars/trucks, and pets. Floats roll and marching bands play in this canine mini-Mardi Gras (no throws allowed; too many retrievers!) During the day, the historic Highland parks are filled with bands, food wagons, and people and pets grooving to the sounds. It's all in good fun for this annual fundraiser for local animal shelters. Look for the annual event around the third week in May.

dodahday.org

TIP

If you want to participate, be sure to dress up yourself and the pup. The competition for the wackiest is stiff!

MAKE THE MAGIC CITY ART CONNECTION,
BRIDGING PEOPLE TO ART

For three days every April, art takes over. Magic City Art Connection is Birmingham's largest festival, with 200 artists exploding with creativity and thousands who come to appreciate their work. The competition is juried, attracting major artists. The great majority are visual artists, but the other arts appear in dances and musical performances. The sensual experience morphs with alluring aromas of special tastings. Food vendors bring their favorites and their most innovative fare. Complete the sensory experience by touching the sculpture installations. This festival propelled Birmingham into Top Ten Best Downtowns in 2014 by Livability.com. Stroll through the displays engaging fully in art.

magiccityart.com

SHHHH ...
FIND THE SECRET STAGES

More than 60 bands will grace the stages, making Secret Stages not so secret. Secret Stages Music Discovery Festival took up the banner of indie music and up-and-coming new artists who are seeking an audience. Fans pour into town to hear new tunes, making Birmingham a well-rounded music destination. Local band St. Paul and the Broken Bones launched here and credits the spotlight of Secret Stages for its propulsion onto the national scene. Secret Stages often discovers new talent on the verge of acclaim. The bands play in a two-block radius of downtown Birmingham, making it easy to stage-hop. The two-day festival takes over the Loft District the first weekend in August.

secretstages.net

PARTY WITH GUSTO
AT THE GREEK FESTIVAL

During the rush to build the Magic City, Greek immigrants poured into the new city. Many of them opened restaurants, many still owned by their descendants. Every September, the food and music draw thousands to the Holy Cross-Holy Trinity Greek Orthodox Cathedral Greek Festival. It's a thoroughly Greek party in mid-September, with all the exuberance brought from the old country in full force on the parking lot stage. Church members dance, play music, and sing in the Greek tradition, with children's performances especially charming. Meanwhile, long lines of people queue up for tasty meals. With so many restaurateurs, the church serves an astounding array of traditional dishes and even mans a drive-through window. In the makeshift shop area, authentic Greek and Mediterranean gifts and Christian souvenirs are available for purchase.

307 19th St. S, 205-716-3088
birminghamgreekfestival.net

EMBRACE YOUR INNER TACKY
AT THE WACKY TACKY LIGHT TOURS

Come dressed as Cousin Eddie. Or Mrs. Claus. Wear your tackiest Christmas sweater. Hop on the bus to see the best of the worst and the wackiest Christmas-time light displays! Join Fresh Air Family for this anti-Norman Rockwell Christmas tradition—the Wacky Tacky Holiday Light Tour. More than a thousand people annually load up on buses for a guided tour of over-the-top Christmas displays. And other holidays—see the Hanukkah House, where they took a Joy to the World decoration and whacked off the "J." Or Santa's Trailer Park, where giant, mooning Santas greet you on the walking path. It is a tactacular event that raises scholarship money for children and youth to go to Gross Out Camp, an award-winning science camp.

freshairfamily.org

TIP

Gather enough people to fill up your own party bus. Bus sizes range from 13 to 35 passengers.

Talladega Superspeedway
Photo courtesy of Mark Peavy

SPORTS AND RECREATION

ACCELERATE
TO TALLADEGA SUPERSPEEDWAY

The legendary Talladega Superspeedway is the biggest, fastest, and hardest-to-win racetrack for cars rocketing at top speed. To sound like a true fan, call it 'Dega. Thousands of people camp in the infield for the social event of the year, which doubles as NASCAR's greatest sporting event. Careers have been made and broken at 'Dega as drivers tempt the treacherous turns and heavy competition. So many people come in through the Talladega airport, it becomes the nation's busiest one weekend each year. Stroll through the infield throng of people, BBQ grills, parties, reunions, and entertainers—people watching can almost surpass in outrageousness the excessive speed on the track. While there, take a track tour and visit the International Motorsports Hall of Fame, where rare car displays and driver tributes celebrate the sport. Opt for a driving experience of your own.

3366 Speedway Blvd., Lincoln, 855-518-7223
Guest services: 256-761-4976
talladegasuperspeedway.com

GET YOUR MOTOR RUNNING
AT BARBER MOTORSPORTS

Yes, a replica of the lost Captain America bike from *Easy Rider* throttles down here. One man's passion drove him to become the world's largest collector of motorcycles. The Barber Motorsports Museum displays more than 1,500 motorcycles, stretching across 100 years of the two-wheeled wonders. In the historic section, early attempts at motorcycles, such as adapting bikes and even carriages, detail the beginnings of the crotch rockets seen on the level above. Rare cars and race cars line the first two floors. Designed in an ever-rising circle like the legendary Guggenheim Museum, the gleaming machines stun with their beauty and design. The museum sits beside an active motor track where cars and motorcycles race to victory throughout the year. Adjoining the track, the Porsche Driving Experience puts you in the driver's seat.

6040 Barber Motorsports Pkwy., Leeds, 205-298-9040
barberracingevents.com

TIP
The Barber Vintage Festival occurs in early October. Famed riders will be on hand along with racing, motorcycle shows, and riding demos.

PLAY BALL
AT REGIONS FIELD/CLASSIC AT RICKWOOD

Taking a seat in Rickwood Field, you can almost hear the crack of Babe Ruth's bat as he knocks a home run over the right-field stands. Satchel Paige and Dizzy Dean threw pitches, and Willie Mays ran for first base, along with 107 other Hall of Famers who played here. Now the oldest ballpark in America, Rickwood still hosts local college and high school games. It celebrates its history annually at the Rickwood Classic, where players and the audience dress in period costumes for an afternoon of nostalgia. In 2013, the Birmingham Barons moved downtown into Regions Field. The new ballpark features a view of the downtown skyline and a 360-degree concourse while keeping the intimate feel of the old Rickwood.

Rickwood Field
1137 2nd Ave. W, 205-458-8161
rickwood.com

Regions Field
1401 1st Ave. S, 205-988-3200
milb.com/birmingham/ballpark/regions-field

BE BULLISH
ON BIRMINGHAM

In a city where no one has ever seen a frozen pond, a hockey team skates past. The Birmingham Bulls, members of the Southern Professional Hockey League, plow the ice at the Pelham Civic Center. After its reboot in 2017, the gutsy young team advanced to compete in the playoffs by 2019. They nearly snatched the title from the defending champion. Another professional sports team in town is Legion, stars of that other football sport: soccer. Birmingham teams, no matter the sport, are hard to beat—Legion also advanced to the playoffs in its first two seasons. Fans can see them play in the new Protective Stadium downtown. The fast pace of these two sports excite and engage a city known for football fans—with hockey and soccer enthusiasts.

500 Amphitheater Rd., Pelham, 205-620-6870
bullshockey.net

2213 1st Ave. S, 205-600-4696
bhmlegion.com

WALK WHERE
LEGENDS LIVE ON

Paul "Bear" Bryant, Bart Starr, Jesse Owens, Willie Mays, Hank Aaron, Mia Hamm, Bo Jackson—the list of famous Alabama athletes and coaches goes on and on. The Alabama Sports Hall of Fame (ASHF) contains 6,000 pieces of sports memorabilia commemorating its accomplished sons and daughters. ASHF is one of the largest sports hall of fame museums in the nation. While Alabama's legendary gridiron players dominate the honorees, athletes from almost every sport are recognized, such as Ray Scott, bass fishing; Charlie Boswell, a blind golfer; Bobby Allison, NASCAR; Jennifer Chandler, diving; Arnold "Swede" Umbach, wrestling; Charles Barkley, basketball; JoJo Starbuck, ice skating; Vonetta Flowers, bobsled; and Evander Holyfield, boxing. Each honoree is represented by mementos and lists of their accomplishments.

2150 Richard Arrington Jr. Blvd. N, 205-323-6665
ashof.org

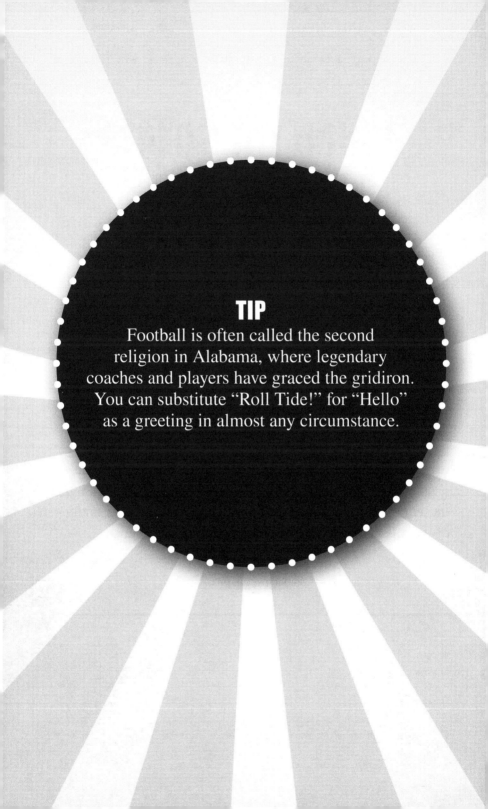

TIP
Football is often called the second religion in Alabama, where legendary coaches and players have graced the gridiron. You can substitute "Roll Tide!" for "Hello" as a greeting in almost any circumstance.

HONOR THE GREATS
AT THE NEGRO SOUTHERN LEAGUE MUSEUM

When baseball became America's pastime in the last century, it caught Birmingham's passion. Leagues popped up everywhere: industrial leagues, church leagues, women's leagues, and minor league teams for white and Black players. Seemingly, everyone who could hold a bat played ball. This intense focus on the sport created a pipeline from Birmingham to the Negro American League and Negro National League. Famed players, such as Leroy "Satchel" Paige and Willie Mays, played for the legendary Black Barons. The Negro Southern League Museum contains the largest collection of original Negro League artifacts. A salute to Alabama's own Bo Jackson applauds a man who played major league baseball and football. Top researchers work with the museum to enhance the collection and promote understanding of the role the leagues played in transcending barriers.

120 16th St. S, 205-581-3040
birminghamnslm.org

● ●

FEAST ON FOOTBALL, FOOD, AND FUN
AT THE MAGIC CITY CLASSIC

Alabama and Auburn may have the biggest rivalry in the nation, but in Alabama, Alabama A&M University (AAMU) and Alabama State University (ASU) rival their rivalry as the two largest historically Black colleges and universities (HBCUs) clash. Their long-running, annual face-off has grown into the highest attendance of an HBCU game and the country's biggest predominantly African American event. More than 200,000 people join the fun at the Magic City Classic at Legion Field. While 60,000 people crowd the stands, even more are barbecuing and tailgating in one of the biggest reunion parties in football. Everybody wins during the week of festivities. The battle of the bands pits ASU's Mighty Marching Hornets against AAMU's Maroon and White Marching Band in a triumphant, on-field musical extravaganza. A parade, pep rally, block parties, and comedy show add to the high spirits of the event.

400 Graymont Ave. W, 205-254-2391
magiccityclassic.com

TEE OFF
AT ROBERT TRENT JONES
GOLF COURSES

Dr. David Bronner, the visionary leader of the Retirement Systems of Alabama, set out to create local tourist attractions. He partnered with famed golf course designer Robert Trent Jones to design a trail from the mountains to the beaches. The Ross Bridge course is woven into the rolling hills of the Shannon Valley, creating one of the longest courses in the world. Styled in the manner of an old parkland course, 10 holes border two lush lakes. The quiet waters are deceptive—they connect with a magnificent 80-foot-drop waterfall. Generous greens lure golfers to try their skills on approach shots. The adjoining resort invites plenty of bragging on a successful game, with restaurants, bars, and a complete pro shop—and a spa for those missed swings.

4000 Grand Ave., Hoover, 205-949-3085
rtjgolf.com/rossbridge

TIP
Start at the mountainous top of the state or start at the southern beaches—either way, you can play your way through the whole system.

SET YOUR COMPASS
FOR OAK MOUNTAIN STATE PARK

The hiking, camping, fishing, swimming, and canoeing bring throngs of people to Oak Mountain State Park. A golf course, horse barn, trails, and a BMX track combine to appeal to those who like both slow and speedy sports. However, the mountain biking and orienteering make Oak Mountain famous. The Double Oak Trail, built by mountain bikers, is one of 52 places worldwide listed as an Epic Ride. The 26-mile trail climbs 1,900 feet with tight single-track and five miles of loop double-track paths. With two mountain ridges and diverse landscapes, Oak Mountain ranks among the best places to go orienteering. A competitive sport, orienteering is essentially a race using a map and a compass. Afterward, spread out a picnic on one of the many tables or under shady trees.

200 Terrace Dr., Pelham, 205-620-2524
alapark.com/oak-mountain-state-park
vulcanorienteering.org

TIP
Bring your own compass and wear good shoes as it is so tempting to get into the racing spirit as you rush to find the electronic punching points.

CANOE THE CAHABA,
SWIM IN A SWIMMING HOLE

A river runs through it. Birmingham is bordered by one of the last free-flowing rivers in Alabama, the Cahaba. In spite of urban sprawl, this feisty little river persists in being one of the most biodiverse rivers in the US. Home to a whopping 131 species of fish, the Cahaba is home to more varieties than are found in all of California. It is possible to get in the water below a highway bridge and feel as though you are in the wilderness after just a few paddle strokes. The most popular time to go is in May, when the rare and beautiful Cahaba Lily blooms in the shoals of the river. Big and white, these put on a spectacular show. Helena and Bibb County are popular put-in spots. For summer, visit Turkey Creek Nature Preserve, where rare fish swim in crystal-clear waters.

TIP
The Blue Hole at Turkey Creek has a natural waterslide slipping you into a swimming hole.

Canoe the Cahaba
2370 Hwy. 52, Helena, 205-874-5623

Cahaba River Society
205-322-5326
cahabariversociety.org/events/category/events/canoe

Turkey Creek Nature Preserve
3906 Turkey Creek Rd., Pinson, 205-680-4116
turkeycreeknp.com

GET ROLLING
AT RAILROAD PARK

Pass by what was once a decrepit railroad dump and see people walking, tossing Frisbees, picnicking, and relaxing. Once an eyesore, Railroad Park transformed into a stunning, award-winning public park. This new oasis looks out onto the city skyline through a lake, 600 trees, and nine acres of lawn. This is far from a barren grassland. Native plants dot the pathways, and a wetland attracts noisy, colorful birds. Memories of the old site remain in benches made from repurposed materials, and in handmade bricks and cobblestones placed throughout. Come here for a stroll, for the playground, to hear a band, or for a movie night. What you will see are families and friends enjoying a park that doubles as a catalyst for Birmingham's downtown renaissance.

1600 1st Ave. S, 205-521-9933
railroadpark.org

TRUNKS ARE UP
AT AVONDALE PARK

Miss Fancy, an elephant, once dominated Avondale Park, where the original zoo was housed. This historic park saved Birmingham's founding fathers when they discovered the underground springs provided the only clean water during a cholera epidemic that threatened to pull the curtain on the Magic City. It is the site of Birmingham's only Civil War skirmish in 1865, when a few Union soldiers stopped to water their horses and were met by a local guard. Only the lady who owned the property received a bullet wound. Today, the spring feeds a duck pond, the fields host art shows, and the amphitheater hosts jazz concerts and theater performances. Instead of riding high on Miss Fancy's back, today's children play in the ball fields and tennis courts. Marriages, reunions, and special events are celebrated in the restored villa.

4101 5th Ave. S, 205-254-2556
birminghamal.gov/parks-and-recreation

TIP
After you enjoy the park, step across the street to the Avondale entertainment district. You will find restaurants, pubs, live music, a brewery, and even a speakeasy!

SPRING FOR SNOWFLAKES
IN ALDRIDGE GARDENS

Hydrangeas call Alabama home. The state grows more hydrangeas in number and species than any other place in the world. Much of the credit for this botanical achievement goes to Eddie Aldridge, who dedicated his career to finding, cultivating, and spreading the beautiful and fragrant blooms to gardens everywhere. He discovered and patented a giant ball of flowers: the Snowflake Hydrangea. There is no better place to enjoy a late spring hydrangea tour than Eddie's personal garden: Aldridge Gardens, which he donated to the City of Hoover. The blooms display a wide spectrum of color and shape throughout the garden. Sculpture and other art grace nature's own palette. Events and classes enhance the experience of this free public garden.

530 Lorna Rd., Hoover, 205-682-8019
aldridgegardens.com

TIP
The hydrangeas tend to bloom in late spring, which is the best time to go.

FOLLOW THE IRON ROAD
AT RED MOUNTAIN PARK

Red Mountain Park forms the western end of a future greenway stretching across Birmingham from end to end. This former mining site now reverberates, not with blasting and hauling carts, but with wind whispering in the trees and birds singing its praises. There is plenty of nature to explore in its 1,500 acres; Red Mountain offers a peek into the blasting past with old mining structures and artifacts. For those who find it difficult to see or hear the beauty, the Butler Snow Sensory Trail offers a way for old and young alike to enjoy the park. It offers 14 activities, a comfort zone, and swinging benches. Some come to relax with four-footed friends at Remy's Dog Park. History also awaits at three historic iron ore mining sites at this free-entry park.

2011 Frankfurt Dr., 205-202-6043
redmountainpark.org

LEARN A BOULDER WAY TO LIVE
AT MOSS ROCK PRESERVE

Rock climbers love the boulder field, and hikers love the forest and streams. As you enter Moss Rock Preserve, the large and varied boulders and outcroppings appeal to climbers of all skill levels. Many expert climbers cut their teeth on these ancient formations. For the casual hiker, the natural beauty engages the senses with waterfalls, wildlife, and the delicate scent of wildflowers in bloom. On a relatively short walk, you can pass through a hardwood forest, a pine forest, an open-brush habitat, and a wetland, all bursting with unique plants and wildlife. The shining star is a blazing star and a rare rayless goldenrod—a total of four rare species dwell on a type of sandstone glade found only in the northeast corridor of Alabama.

617 Preserve Pkwy., Hoover
hooveral.org

HAVE A BLOOMING GOOD TIME
AT THE BIRMINGHAM BOTANICAL GARDENS

Walking the high path of the Wildflower Garden in early spring, you might think it snowed during the night, but no, the bloodroots are blooming! The scent of cherry blossoms fills the air in the renowned Japanese Garden, which features an authentic tea house built by an honored master. Colors explode in the Rhododendron Garden. More than 3,000 plant varieties flourish year-round in 25 garden collections. Always free, open 365 days from sunrise to sunset, the Birmingham Botanical Gardens serve as a perpetual oasis. Educational programs enhance the experience, with classes in native plants, herbs, flower arranging, pruning, gardening, and photography. Check out the only public botanical library in the US.

2612 Lane Park Rd., 205-414-3950
bbgardens.org

HORN IN ON A ROARING GOOD TIME
AT THE BIRMINGHAM ZOO

Elephants have trumpeted throughout Birmingham's history! First, Miss Fancy carried children through Avondale Park. Then Mona arrived at the zoo in 1955. Today, the Birmingham Zoo honors its pachyderm past with national leadership in elephant conservation. The Trails of Africa blend species with a bachelor elephant herd, red river hogs, rhinos, and more. These animals are among 950 living at the zoo, representing 230 species. The exhibits include primates, big cats, sea lions, birds, amphibians, reptiles, and insects. Several of the animals, such as rhinos, are endangered. Don't miss the pirate train ride on the Birmingham Zoo Express. Animal lovers can schedule behind-the-scenes tours and personalized encounters with a giraffe.

2630 Cahaba Rd., 205-879-0409
birminghamzoo.com

AMP THE AMPHIBIANS
AT THE SALAMANDER FESTIVAL

As part of one of the top five states in biodiversity, Birmingham celebrates its rare creatures. The Salamander Festival celebrates a particularly beautiful spotted salamander. After the first warm rain on the edge of winter, these little amphibians migrate down to the creek. When they arrive, a complex mating dance begins, with yellow spots flashing under the water. Every January, the Friends of Shades Creek celebrate the little lovers with live animal presentations, costumed players, music, and of course, dancing. To get a closer look, they lead hikes up to the salamander's habitat under old logs and leaf litter. The stars of the festival will be on hand for adults and children to hold and admire.

shadescreek.org

Artist Joe Minter
Photo courtesy of Mark Peavy

CULTURE
AND HISTORY

VULCAN, THE GOD OF THE FORGE,
WATCHES OVER US

Towering above the city, Vulcan perpetually examines the spear he just pulled from the forge. As the world's largest cast-iron statue, Vulcan emerged from the forge himself in 1904. He was created by city leaders for the 1904 World's Fair in St. Louis, crafted to represent the young steel town. He captured the Grand Prize in the Palace of Mines and Metallurgy. Vulcan returned to the city of his birth in pieces. Due to his bare backside, the ladies of Birmingham rebuffed attempts to erect him in a downtown park. He spent several years at the Alabama State Fairgrounds before a Works Progress Administration project built his sandstone pedestal atop Red Mountain. Today, visitors can ride to the top of his base for a panoramic view of the area. A museum tracks the history of Vulcan and the city that created him.

1701 Valley View Dr., 205-933-1409
visitvulcan.com

EXPERIMENT
AT THE McWANE SCIENCE CENTER

An old, shuttered department store reemerged as the McWane Science Center in downtown Birmingham. Since it opened in 1998, millions of people have visited the center, stretching out on a bed of nails, touching live stingrays, and staring into the gaping mouth of an Alabama Mosasaur, the most feared prehistoric sea monster. As the site of an ancient ocean and swamps teeming with life, Alabama hides more dinosaur bones beneath its surface than any other state east of the Mississippi. At McWane, you can see dinosaur bones and fossils found nearby. The Itty Bitty Magic City spurs creative learning in preschool children. Along the way, children can explore space, bubbles, the science of the whishing sound of a basketball, and antigravity. Education programs engage guests with experiments and demonstrations. The IMAX Dome Theater plays documentaries using technology that brings the audience into the action.

200 19th St. N, 205-714-8300
mcwane.org

DIG THE TIME
BEFORE DINOSAURS ROAMED

Fossils older and rarer than dinosaur bones are found at one of the top three Coal Age fossil sites in the world, once an ancient swamp. Giant amphibians, reptiles, and water creatures lived in the soaked earth on the border of a 300-million-year-old sea. The Union Chapel Mine produced coal for decades and was set for reclamation when the rare fossils were discovered. The area is famous for being the only known site where a full track record of the ancient horseshoe crab is found. The largest creature, an Attenosaurus, left tracks as large as a human hand. The fossils are easily found and children as young as five years old have found museum-quality pieces, which they can keep unless the fossil is significant to science. Prep by visiting the collection at the McWane Science Center. Groups such as Fresh Air Family host paleontologist-led hunts.

freshairfamily.org

TIP
Bring a small hammer and a screwdriver to ease out your finds. Most can just be picked up from the slag pile.

ENTER BIRMINGHAM'S ANTEBELLUM PAST
AT ARLINGTON

A sword hangs in a case, a testimony to love. The Civil War soldier dug his sword into a tree, declaring his undying love to his weeping betrothed as long as the sword remained. He never returned. The red iron ore throughout Birmingham colors the soil, creating poor farmland, so few plantations existed in the area. Arlington Antebellum Home & Gardens stands as the last reminder of the Old South. The Greek Revival home showcases 19th-century decorative arts with furniture, textiles, silver, and paintings. The garden is planted with heirloom plants. An early owner, William S. Mudd, may be related to the notorious Dr. Mudd who reset the leg of John Wilkes Booth. The house was occupied by Union Major General James H. Wilson, who spared it from the soldier's torch because Mudd was a fellow Mason.

331 Cotton Ave. SW, 205-780-5656
arlingtonantebellumhomeandgardens.com

MEET THE SPIRITS
WHO HAUNT US

London had Jack the Ripper, but Birmingham can claim Hatchet Harry. In a dark alley, ghost hunters claim to have seen shadows of his signature hat and hatchet. Others claim to have met Colonel Edward Tutwiler down in the kitchen of the historic hotel. Hank Williams, the prolific country singer and songwriter, still plays in his old room at the Redmont Hotel, the last place he was seen alive. If a ghost tour is too grisly, try the brothels and madams tour of the leading ladies of Birmingham's early mining days. Or explore the civil-rights history tour. The Birmingham Historic Touring Company, led by Wolfgang Poe, offers insights into the history, architecture, and colorful characters who shaped the Magic City.

205-440-2720
bhamhistory.com

HEAR STORIES
COME ALIVE
AT OAK HILL CEMETERY

Meet Louise Wooster, the colorful madam who saved the young city of Birmingham during a cholera epidemic. Or greet Charles Linn, a city pioneer, who wanted to wake up on Judgment Day looking out over the greatest industrial city in the South. Perhaps famous murder victims Emma, May, and Irene Hawes haunt the cemetery, looking for the husband/father who committed a sensational crime in 1888. Oak Hill Cemetery frequently offers guided tours on Saturdays to introduce visitors to Birmingham's buried history. In the fall, around Halloween, the dead come to life with local actors embodying the most fascinating residents of the city's first cemetery. In June, it hosts a film festival featuring historic reels and independent movies.

120 19th St. N, 205-251-6532
oakhillbiringham.com

PICTURE CENTURIES OF BEAUTY
AT THE BIRMINGHAM MUSEUM OF ART

The ever-inspiring Renaissance launched a new art museum when 29 Italian paintings from the Samuel H. Kress Foundation were first exhibited here in 1952. The Birmingham Museum of Art has since grown to house more than 26,000 art objects, making it one of the finest regional museums in the country. Its holdings span from ancient to modern works, with a broad cultural diversity from Asia, Europe, Africa, and the Americas. Decorative arts embellish its collection with what is considered the nation's finest assortment of Vietnamese ceramics, plus superior collections of English ceramics and French furniture. A local couple provided the perfect addition: the largest collection of Wedgwood outside of England, beautifully interpreted in its displays. The museum is owned by the City of Birmingham, allowing free entry for all who want to experience it. Education programs offer lectures, music, classes, special events, and artist presentations.

2000 Rev. Abraham Woods Jr. Blvd., 205-254-2565
artsbma.org

TIP
An entire room is dedicated to children's activities. Check it out with your little ones.

PREPARE FOR A SENSORY OVERLOAD
AT JOE MINTER'S YARD

Protest signs and Jesus mix comfortably in the African village created by artist Joe Minter. Sculptures, shrines, wooden plaques, and baby dolls in his urban yard tell the story of his people, from their arrival on slave ships to modern-day police abuse. The stories emerge with the help of work gloves, car parts, bicycle chains, metal frames, wood, and Christmas decorations. The famed folk artist crafts moving testimonies to the struggle for equality and the importance of his Christian faith. A stroll through the maze of yard art combines a sensory experience of beauty and thought. Even the art cannot compare with meeting the artist himself, a fascinating free spirit and creative mind working on "orders from God."

931 Nassau Ave. SW, 205-322-7370
facebook.com/joeminterafricanvillage

TIP
The artist will come out and give you a grand tour if he is home. It is appreciated if you show your appreciation for this folk artist with a tip.

TRACE THE ROAD TO FREEDOM
ON THE CIVIL RIGHTS TRAIL

It began at Bethel, which starts the story of the Birmingham Civil Rights Movement, a historic struggle fought in the streets, parks, and churches. The Rev. Fred Shuttlesworth championed rights from the pulpit of Bethel and sought help from the Rev. Dr. Martin Luther King Jr., a fellow pastor from Montgomery. Their leadership clashed with Jim Crow enforcers to dramatic effect, bringing about an end to segregation laws. Reminders of the struggle can be seen in Kelly Ingram Park, where statues capture the fire hoses, dog attacks, jailed children, praying pastors, and Dr. King. Across the street, the Birmingham Civil Rights Institute (BCRI) leads you from displays of a segregated world to today's struggle for human rights. Across from the BCRI stands the 16th Street Baptist Church, where protest songs pierced the air, speeches inspired marchers, and the Children's March poured out of the sanctuary. In a final act of depravity, a bomb here ended the lives of four little girls, sparking the passage of the Civil Rights Act. The area was designated a national monument by President Barack Obama in 2017.

heritagetrail.birminghamal.gov

Birmingham Civil Rights Institute
520 16th St. N, 205-328-9696
bcri.org

Bethel Baptist Church
3200 28th Ave. N, 205-322-5360
bethelcollegeville.org

16th Street Baptist Church
1530 6th Ave. N, 205-251-9402
16thstreetbaptist.org

TIP

Start your exploration of the Civil Rights Trail
at Bethel Baptist Church. Call ahead to book
their historian for a tour. She lived through the
struggle and shares her personal experience to
help you understand the climate that birthed the
civil-rights movement.

HAVE A BLAST
AT SLOSS FURNACES

In the hills surrounding Birmingham, the fires from Sloss Furnaces would light up the night sky. From 1882 to 1971, Sloss Furnaces produced pig iron, so called because of the shallow connectors between the molds, giving it the appearance of a pig's tail. These furnaces produced 24,000 tons of high-quality iron the first year. Birmingham is one of the only places in the world where everything you need to make steel is found within 30 miles. Colonel James Sloss helped found the Magic City with his railroad connections and new blast furnaces. When the operation shut down, the city moved to develop the site into the only preserved blast furnace in the US. Now it's a National Historic Landmark, and you can explore Sloss with self-guided tours. Watch out for ghosts! Sloss often hosts concerts, cookoffs, and paranormal events from ghost stories to ghostbusting investigations.

20 32nd St. N, 205-254-2025
slossfurnaces.com

TIP
Be sure to walk into the engine rooms to see the massive machinery it took to make pig iron (named for the mold that resembled the animal).

TAKE OFF
AT THE SOUTHERN MUSEUM OF FLIGHT

No one believed African American men could fly airplanes during World War II until the Tuskegee Airmen proved them wrong. See the story of these brave and pioneering pilots in an exhibition at the Southern Museum of Flight. The disastrous Bay of Pigs invasion in 1961 took the lives of four men from the Alabama Air National Guard. Sixty men from Alabama trained Cuban exiles for an invasion of Cuba. These men are honored in the Aviation Hall of Fame in the Southern Museum of Flight. Other exhibits include Korean War jets, Vietnam-era helicopters, and crop-dusters. Throughout the museum, you can see memorabilia from military, civilian, and experimental aircraft from the earliest days of powered flight to modern times.

4343 73rd St. N, 205-833-8226
southernmuseumofflight.org

TIP
Check the website for the occasional plane-building activities for children.

FEEL YOUNG AGAIN
AT THE SAMUEL ULLMAN MUSEUM

A former Confederate soldier, Samuel Ullman fought for the rights of African American children to receive the same education as whites. Serving on Birmingham's first school board, he also argued for equal pay for Black teachers. The German-born Jew served as a lay rabbi for Temple Emanu-El, a Reform congregation, but he is most famous for his retirement occupation as a poet. In 1918, at the age of 78, he penned the poem "Youth," a testament to optimism and youthful outlook. A framed copy of the poem hung in the office of one of Ullman's biggest fans, General Douglas MacArthur, when he was stationed in Japan. The war-weary Japanese embraced the poem as they began to rebuild their country. The former Ullman residence was opened in 1994 by the Japan-America Society of Alabama and the University of Alabama at Birmingham.

2150 15th Ave. S, 205-910-3876
uab.edu/ullmanmuseum

NO TUXEDO REQUIRED
AT THE ALABAMA JAZZ HALL OF FAME

In Birmingham, Tuxedo Junction was a place immortalized forever by a song cowritten by Alabama Jazz Hall of Fame honoree Erskine Hawkins. His legendary Parker High School teacher, John T. "Fess" Whatley, provided a feeder for bands such as Duke Ellington and Count Basie. More than a dozen famed jazz musicians graduated from his program. One of his students, the eccentric Herman "Sun Ra" Blount, formed his Intergalactic Infinity Arkestra. Jazz greats with ties to Alabama include Montgomery's Nat King Cole, Florence's W. C. Handy, Troy's Clarence "Pinetop" Smith, and Birmingham's Lionel Hampton. The art-deco Carver Theater in the Civil Rights District houses a collection of artifacts. A living museum, the Carver often rings with music by way of jazz jam sessions, concerts, classes, and dances.

1631 4th Ave. N, 205-327-9424
jazzhall.com

WATCH PERFECTION MADE PERFECT
AT VIRGINIA SAMFORD THEATRE

The opening curtain rose in 1927 for what is now known as the Virginia Samford Theatre in Caldwell Park. After too many of its actors departed for World War II, it closed, reopening in 1950 as Town and Gown, led by the legendary James Hatcher. He demanded perfection: that every hand hit the same height and every knee bend at the same angle. This larger-than-life character developed local talent into Broadway and film careers, most notably actress and author Fannie Flagg. Today, the historic theater continues to offer a broad range of dance, music, and theater performances. In keeping with the Hatcher philosophy, the theater educates young people in the art and discipline of the stage. From classics to new works, the theater both challenges and entertains through art.

1116 26th St. S, 205-251-1206
virginiasamfordtheatre.org

GRASP THE EDGE OF YOUR SEAT
AT BIRMINGHAM FESTIVAL THEATRE

Located on what was once a loading dock, Birmingham Festival Theatre persevered to become the city's longest continuously operating community theater. The intimate theater has staged more than 250 productions seen by more than 100,000 people. Birmingham Festival Theatre spans from new wave to classics in its repertoire, with the city's finest talent. The productions continue to inspire with edgy new or rarely performed productions, along with original debuts from local writers. This historic theater keeps the laughter and the tears rolling in this quaint setting in the Five Points South entertainment center. Its season can range from the LGBTQ-based play *Significant Other* to *Sordid Lives*, a classic Southern gothic comedy.

1901½ 11th Ave. S, 205-933-2383
bftonline.org

PUT A SONG IN YOUR HEART
AT RED MOUNTAIN THEATRE

Patsy Cline, the Lennon Sisters, and Tevye from *Fiddler on the Roof* have all been given voice at Red Mountain Theatre Company. This venue recruits Tony winners to perform alongside local talent and acting students, merging them into thrilling musical performances. Here, local writers debut new works and up-and-coming directors hone their craft. A season could include everything from an old favorite to a challenging new work. One of the goals of the theater is to engage the community with both thought-provoking art and also a place to escape the problems of life with a song, a dance, and a laugh or two. With an active education program, Red Mountain Theatre pulls from an impressive talent pool of its own making.

1600 3rd Ave. S, 205-324-2424
redmountaintheatre.org

ACT RIGHT
FOR THE CHILDREN

The audience may not be old, but the acting company is. Founded in 1947, Birmingham Children's Theater (BCT) is one of the oldest and largest theater companies for young audiences in the country. Shows range from *E.L.V.E.S.: The Experience* to *Zombie Thoughts*. You can count on seeing the classics as well: *Peter Pan*, *The Wizard of Oz*, and *Seussical the Musical* have been performed in recent years. Some of the most exciting offerings are the locally based stories such as *The Watsons Go to Birmingham—1963* and *Tuxedo Junction*. Children and their families can expect professional performances of the best plays for youngsters. The plays and musicals are entertaining, and a good lesson might slip in from time to time.

Birmingham-Jefferson Convention Center
205-458-8181
bct123.org

Alabama Goods

SHOPPING
AND FASHION

LOCAL IS GREAT
AT ALABAMA GOODS

Creativity abounds in Alabama and can be found in a unique shop filled with items made exclusively by local artists, artisans, and cooks. Sherry Hartley and Beth Staula founded Alabama Goods based on their love of their home state and their passion for sharing its unique culture. Here, you can find famed Alabama white sauce, handcrafted cutting boards shaped like the state, and red dirt T-shirts dyed in iron-ore-tinted clay. Items ranging from botanical-inspired earrings to clever tea towels to paintings fill the walls and tables. Handmade soaps, pottery, and scarves sit in front of the store, while chocolates, cheese straws, hot sauces, and muscadine juice line the gourmet offerings in the rear. The works of local authors document more about the city and state for visitors and history buffs.

2933 18th St. S, Homewood, 205-803-3900
alabamagoods.com

TIP
This store carries the best tea towels for that handy gift. Many of them are beautiful, some showcase local icons, and others are downright funny.

SIP THE SPIRITS
OF THE FIRST LADY OF LIQUOR

The gin splays out in a bathtub as a Prohibition-era joke in LeNell's Beverage Boutique. A shelf holds an entire collection of obscure Black wine and spirit makers' products. A bourbon cabinet holds the familiar and rare, and occasionally the Pappy Van Winkle, a brand the First Lady of Liquor discovered and promoted before it became the premium choice. LeNell Camacho Santa Ana, an Alabama native, made the rounds from Brooklyn to California and Mexico to settle close to home on the outskirts of downtown. Her cinderblock store, next to a Greek Revival mansion, hosts weekly tastings of either new offerings or unusual pairings. Much of LeNell's legendary success is based on her passion for education in the art of the cocktail and training of the palate.

1208 32nd St. N, 205-536-3557
lenells.com

GET SOUTHERN-STYLE GLAM
AT GUS MAYER

If you are coming to a Southern bridal tea, shop at Gus Mayer's for the perfect summer party dress. It will be simple, exquisite, and well-fitted. Helpful clerks will dash about to find alluring accessories. The upscale store opened in 1900 and remains a family-owned business. Gus Mayer isn't just for special occasions. A contemporary collection takes you to the picnic or the ball field to watch Little League. The store presents a study of Birmingham itself, the dichotomy of a Chanel suit with matching hat and a shaggy vest for date night. In between, jewelry, shoes, and cosmetics complete the fashion picture. And you can pick up a perfectly appropriate wedding gift to take to the tea.

225 Summit Blvd., Ste. 700, 205-870-3300
gusmayer.com

FLASH FASHION-FORWARD
AT ETC....

This fashion-forward shop brings in clothing from top designers around the world. And from next door. Birmingham's designer Liz Legg might mix a mammoth bone or a less ancient coin with raw geodes. Or, find vintage Hermes or Rolex. Cathy Waterman, Armenta, Moritz Glik, Monique Pean, Spinelli Kilcollin, and Hoorsenbuhs bring everything from diamonds to bangles. In clothing, a feminine and flirty Rodarte can be polished off with a Golden Goose silver sneaker or a colorful midtop sporting a purple star. Knitwear, ever ready to go onto an island retreat or a stop at the carpool line, comes in unique pieces from Raquel Allegra, Inhabit, Proenza Schouler, and the Great. Fashion at Etc. re-creates itself daily.

2726 Cahaba Rd., Mountain Brook, 205-871-6747
shopetcjewelry.com

GET BACK
TO THE BASIC

Feeling great in your clothes takes on a new dimension at basic. A store based on human rights along with great looks, basic. purchases designs from sources paying decent wages in dignified working conditions. Many of the designers are local, such as Natalie Chanin, a Florence, Alabama native. She hired the sewing ladies left behind by plant closures and created a unique, handmade brand. Joining the slow fashion movement, the clothes are made to last, making consumption more sustainable. The basics include tops for jeans, shirts, and sweaters for day-to-day winter wear. To aid in clothing maintenance, the shop offers classes to those new to sewing needles. The fashion is size-free, offering fits for any body.

2214 2nd Ave. N, (205) 542-7590
abasicshop.com

TIP
Honeycreeper Chocolate shares their space and offers hot chocolates on tap.

GO WHERE COMFORT IS
IN STYLE

He calls it "lived-in luxury." Billy Reid, an internationally known designer, lives in Alabama, where his Southern sensibility shows in his rustic but sophisticated, style. His Birmingham store dwells in an old industrial space with voluminous 24-foot ceilings and exposed bricks. While an icon of fashion, he remains the boy who grew up in his mom's retail shop. He makes clothes people wear every day, not just on an evening out. His clothes for men and women share a modern appeal with a cozy fit. Much like his flagship store in his hometown of Florence, Alabama, the Birmingham shop works to be a center of creativity, where artists and chefs can gather to inspire. Whether he is mixing patterns and graphics or hosting musical artists, Billy Reid is a place to celebrate the senses.

2807 2nd Ave. S, 205-588-4533
billyreid.com

PUT THE MAN BACK
IN MEN'S FASHIONS

It's all about bringing back individual style in menswear. Aisha Taylor focuses on helping men bridge from day to night while staying rooted in their own authenticity. Thus, Bridge + Root offers a wide range of products from cufflinks to colorful socks, from trucker jackets to tuxedo pants, from beard oil to fragrances. Top it all off with a flattering fedora. Aisha translates her years as a stylist into helping men find their fashion way. Her goal is for men to feel comfortable and confident in how they look. Coming into her shop means getting her personal help to coordinate a complete outfit for a special occasion or just being comfy lounging around the house. Women are welcome—for gender-neutral offerings or to replace that high school T-shirt they are tired of seeing on their husband.

2212 Morris Ave., Ste. 200
bridgeandroot.com

STEP BACK INTO OLD-WORLD ELEGANCE
AT SHAIA'S OF HOMEWOOD

With an old-world leather sofa and chairs surrounded by sharp suits and shoes, you get the feeling you might have stepped into Jay Gatsby's dressing room. The warm atmosphere sets a tone more akin to a men's club than a retail shop. Indeed, men bring their sons here to teach them proper dress. Founded in 1922, Shaia's fourth generation recently added a concept shop devoted to fashion geared for a younger crowd. Armani and all the classics can be found, along with a few upstarts. *Esquire* routinely names it in the Best of Class list. The upscale shop can design and create everything from a custom-fit suit to a travel wardrobe to a new home closet to accommodate your threads of investment. Jay Gatsby, indeed.

818 18th St. S, Homewood, 205-871-1312
shaias.com

SPRINKLE YOUR WORLD
WITH FAIRY DUST
AND WHITE FLOWERS

Owners Eric and Diana Hanson fell in love with a magic garden created by artists who first lived in their home. More than just flowers bloomed for this artist and photographer; they began designing custom T-shirts that flourished in the rich soil of showrooms. Soon, they opened their own shop, White Flowers, to showcase their own designs, from baby clothes to tea towels. Entering White Flowers evokes every girl's fantasy of a fairy cottage. Sculptures, drawings, dried flowers, gauzy towers—all in white—tempt you to listen for the galloping of Prince Charming's steed. Clever sayings dot the T-shirts and towels with wisdoms such as, "Wildflowers grow where they will and come back year after year, like a forever friend."

Shops of Grand River, Ste. 688, Leeds, 205-871-4640
whiteflowers.com

GET DOLLED UP
FOR BARBIE'S DREAMHOUSE

It all started with a 1930s Shirley Temple doll for Mary Charles. Living in a home with no radio, before television, her main entertainment was provided by dolls. For decades, dolls have been her livelihood and passion. People from all over the world seek out her doll shop housed in a Homewood cottage. The Mary Charles Doll House sells collectible dolls, new and old, to people in search of that special gift. The shop is one of 10 doll repair shops approved by the Madame Alexander Doll Company. Her customers depend on her expertise in antiques, rarities, dollhouses, and accessories. Her store resembles part retail, part museum. For those girls who wish to give Dolly a tea party, miniature tea sets stand ready to serve.

1901 Oxmoor Rd., Homewood, 205-870-5544
marycharlesdollhouseal.com

TAKE
THE DR. PEPPER CURE

If you know which space to visit, you can enter the vault where the top-secret Dr. Pepper recipe was secured. This former industrial site has morphed into decorator shopping, restaurants, a theater, and a weekend fresh market. While you enjoy the live music and munch on fresh-baked muffins, stroll through local maker booths displaying leather, beadwork, tie-dye, batik, art, pottery, and clothes. You can purchase everything from a watermelon to a bar of soap to a dining room table to a painting. The Saturday-only Pepper Place Market launched as a place to find quality produce and organic products. It has evolved into a weekend staple for entertainment, shopping, and visiting with neighbors. Be sure to bring Fido: Fetch provides an ice cream truck for dogs.

2829 2nd Ave. S
pepperplacemarket.com
pepperplace.com

TIP
Sometimes, you can taste your way to a good breakfast! Be sure to try the goodies offered along the way.

EVERY BOOK IS SIGNED
AT THE ALABAMA BOOKSMITH

Only one bookstore in our known literary universe offers only books signed by the author, Alabama Booksmith. A veteran bookseller from generations of booksellers, owner Jake Reiss transformed a normal bookshop with stuffed racks of books into a collector's dream. Armed with the knowledge that the true book collector focuses on first editions and signed copies, Jake grants the desires of his bookworm patrons. This unique model emphasizing the personal touch shows every book's face—no spine shopping here! While people from all 50 states and all over the world order the signed copies, locals can take their books right from the hand of the author. More than a thousand authors have made the pilgrimage to Alabama Booksmith for the packed signing events.

2626 19th Pl. S, Homewood, 205-870-4242
alabamabooksmith.com

TIP

Readers looking for a book club can chat with the booksellers at Little Professor. The shop both hosts a book club and can recommend others.

MORE BOOKSTORES

Little Professor Bookshop
2844 18th St. S, Homewood, 205-870-7461
littleprofessorhomewood.com

Thank You Books
5502 Crestwood Blvd., Unit B, 205-202-3021
thankyoubookshop.com

Books-A-Million
1624 Gadsden Hwy., Trussville, 205-661-9177
booksamillion.com

Barnes and Noble
201 Summit Blvd., 205-298-0665
171 Main St., Hoover, 205-682-4467
barnesandnoble.com

Church Street Coffee and Books
81 Church St., Mountain Brook, 205-870-2227
churchstreetshop.com

PURCHASE THE PAST
ON THE ALABAMA ANTIQUE TRAIL

Follow the Alabama Antique Trail, with stores for every taste and style. Birmingham is studded with antique stores to fill historic homes and new construction popping up around the city. Some focus on European antiques (Lolo French Antiques et More) while others focus on repurposing in unique ways (Junky to Funky). Some are a collection of sellers, each with a personality all its own (Urban Suburban.) Others create shabby chic by transforming the humble into the spectacular (Oak Mountain Emporium). Collectibles rule in shops such as What's on 2nd. The grande dame of antique shops is Hanna Antiques Mall, with 35 massive cases of jewelry, silver, and collectibles, plus 27,000 square feet of European and American antiques. The Alabama Antique Trail has compiled a list to make it easy to buy memories. Pick up a Trail brochure at any of the shops.

alabamaantiquetrail.com

Lolo French Antiques et More
300 1st Ave. S, 205-323-6033
lolofrenchantiques.com

Junky to Funky
311 Main St., Trussville, 205-537-100
junky2funkyboutique.com

Urban Suburban Antiques
5514 Crestwood Blvd., 205-592-0777
urbansuburbanantiques.net

Irondale Pickers
5401 Beacon Dr., Irondale, 205-407-5166
irondalepickers.com

What's on Second?
1101 20th St. S, 205-322-2688

Oak Mountain Emporium
2700 Pelham Pkwy., Pelham, 205-664-4333

Hanna Antiques Mall
2424 7th Ave. S, 205-323-6036
hannaantiques.com

SHOP A CITY STORE
OLDER THAN THE CITY, BROMBERG'S

The Bromberg family opened their first store before Birmingham was incorporated as a city, making it older than the place it calls home. It is one of the oldest family businesses in America. Opening in 1836, Bromberg's third generation brought the finer things of life to a sleepy town bursting into the Magic City. Bromberg's primarily deals in diamonds and fine jewelry, putting rings on the fingers of thousands of hopeful brides and happy wives. Don't see what you like? The master jeweler can design your dream ring. Once the wedding is set, the gift section helps those who are invited to the happy occasion. Watches, rings, earrings, necklaces, and trained staff make happy occasion or "I'm sorry" shopping easy.

Downtown, The Summit, Mountain Brook Village
brombergs.com

GET YOUR PEANUTS
AT THE PEANUT DEPOT

The rich scent of fresh-roasted peanuts permeates the air even before you enter the building. The Peanut Depot cranks up its antique roasting machines and transforms the average peanut into a delicacy. Just seeing the old machines at work is worth the visit. For more than a hundred years, this company has been honoring the tradition of preparing peanuts without oils or preservatives, making them a healthy, flavorful snack. Three flavors emerge from the fire: fresh-roasted, salted, and Cajun. Depending on your peanut addiction, you can buy a bag of peanuts for yourself, your family, or your stadium. Choose your bag: plastic, burlap, or gift-wrapped for a friend.

3009 Messer Airport Hwy., 205-251-3314
peanutdepot.com

TIP
Roasted peanuts are a traditional treat in the South. Almost half of the peanuts grown in the United States are grown in Alabama. Get some—we have plenty!

REED BOOKS
AND MUSEUM
OF FOND MEMORIES

When Jim Reed's wife decided that their living room should be a place where people could actually sit, she banished her husband's book obsession into what is now Jim Reed Books and Museum of Fond Memories. A confessed hoarder, Jim divides people into keepers and tossers, landing solidly in the keeper lane. His quirky collection resembles a combination of a yard sale and an old bachelor who was never really housebroken. Spending an hour or two with Jim floods the senses with memories, chuckles, and the sense that his shop holds a significant percentage of the world's knowledge. Books range from new to 500 years old. Things range from a giant Porky Pig to vintage lava lamps. If you seek a book, no matter how obscure, Jim can root it out for you.

2021 3rd Ave. N, 205-326-4460
jimreedbooks.com, redclaydiary.com

TIP

Be sure to talk to Jim Reed himself—a delightful and quirky character. You can find his hilarious books in his store to take home.

Vulcan statue
Photo courtesy of Mark Peavy

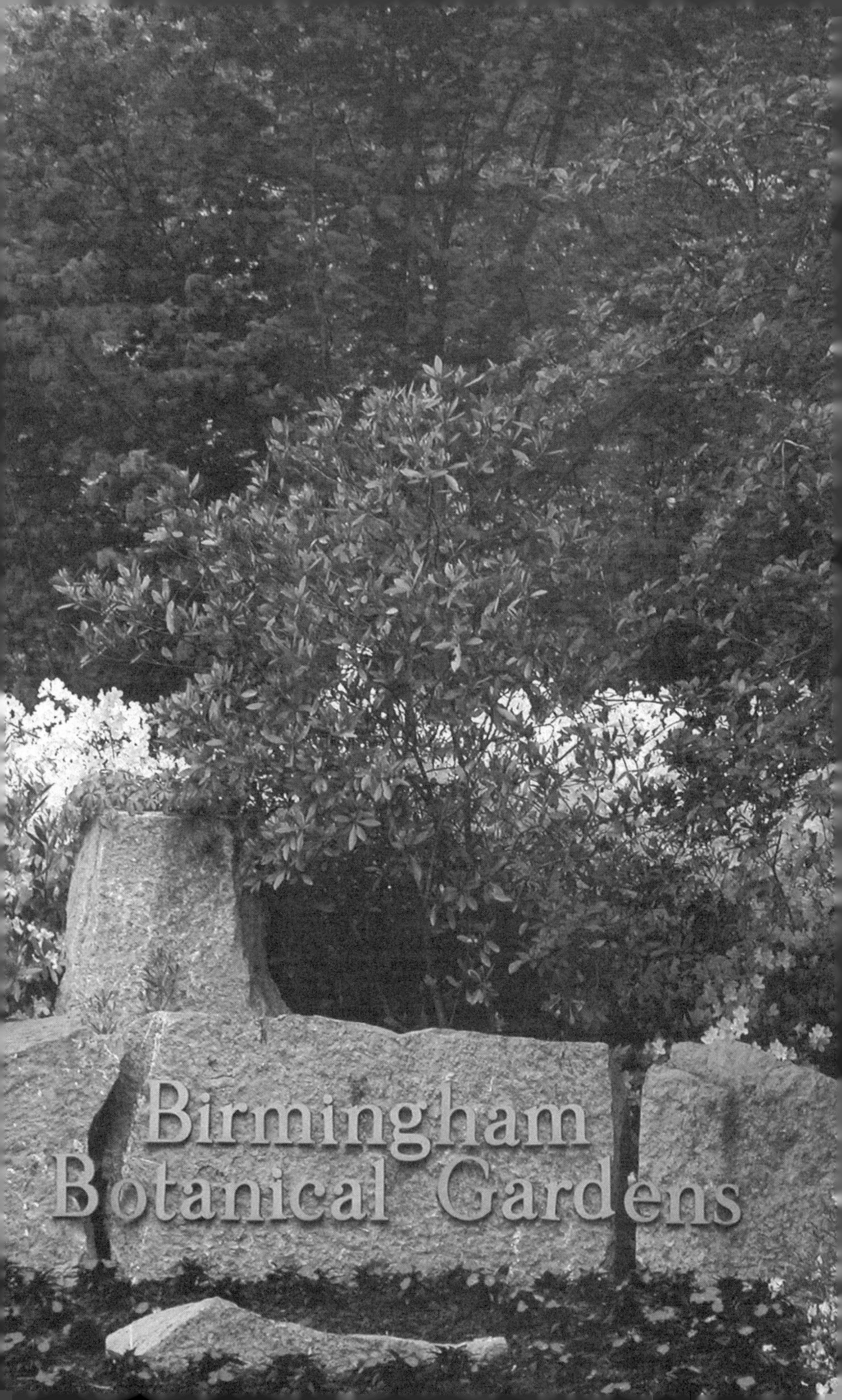
Birmingham
Botanical Gardens

ACTIVITIES
BY SEASON

SUMMER

Canoe the Cahaba, Swim in a Swimming Hole, 74

Set Your Compass for Oak Mountain State Park, 73

Have a Blooming Good Time at the Birmingham Botanical Gardens, 81

Encounter Reel Fun at the Sidewalk Film Fest, 54

Horn In on a Roaring Good Time at the Birmingham Zoo, 82

Experiment at the McWane Science Center, 87

Tune to Colonial with the National Sacred Harp Singing Convention, 55

Have a Blast at Sloss Furnaces, 96

Shhhh . . . Find the Secret Stages, 59

Take the Dr. Pepper Cure, 117

Trunks Are Up at Avondale Park, 77

Tee Off at Robert Trent Jones Golf Courses, 72

Get Rolling at Railroad Park, 76

Picture Centuries of Beauty at the Birmingham Museum of Art, 92

FALL

Hear Stories Come Alive at Oak Hill Cemetery, 91

Enter Birmingham's Antebellum Past at Arlington, 89

Salute Birmingham for Starting Veterans Day Parades, 56

Feast on Football, Food, and Fun at the Magic City Classic, 71

Accelerate to Talladega Superspeedway, 64

Play Ball at Regions Field/Classic at Rickwood, 66

Party with Gusto at the Greek Festival, 60

Horn In on a Roaring Good Time at the Birmingham Zoo, 82

Set Your Compass for Oak Mountain State Park, 73

WINTER

Amp the Amphibians at the Salamander Festival, 83

No Tuxedo Required at the Alabama Jazz Hall of Fame, 99

Every Book Is Signed at the Alabama Booksmith, 118

Soar as High Culture Dances, Sings, and Plays, 34

Enter Birmingham's Antebellum Past at Arlington, 89

Set Your Compass for Oak Mountain State Park, 73

Make Moorish Fun at the Alabama Theater, 52

Picture Centuries of Beauty at the Birmingham Museum of Art, 92

Walk Where Legends Live On, 68

Feel Young Again at the Samuel Ullman Museum, 98

Put a Song in Your Heart at Red Mountain Theatre, 102

Take Off at the Southern Museum of Flight, 97

Embrace Your Inner Tacky at the Wacky Tacky Light Tours, 61

• •

SPRING

Have a Blooming Good Time at the Birmingham Botanical Gardens, 81

Spring for Snowflakes in Aldridge Gardens, 78

Canoe the Cahaba, Swim in a Swimming Hole, 74

Going to the Dogs on Do Dah Day, 57

Drink in an Opera Shot, 35

Make the Magic City Art Connection, Bridging People to Art, 58

Follow the Iron Road at Red Mountain Park, 79

Play Ball at Regions Field/Classic at Rickwood, 66

Tee Off at Robert Trent Jones Golf Courses, 72

SUGGESTED
ITINERARIES

THE GREAT OUTDOORS

Canoe the Cahaba, Swim in a Swimming Hole, 74

Follow the Iron Road at Red Mountain Park, 79

Set Your Compass for Oak Mountain State Park, 73

Learn a Boulder Way to Live at Moss Rock Preserve, 80

Have a Blooming Good Time at the Birmingham Botanical Gardens, 81

Spring for Snowflakes in Aldridge Gardens, 78

Get Rolling at Railroad Park, 76

Trunks Are Up at Avondale Park, 77

Dig the Time before Dinosaurs Roamed, 88

FOR THE VEGETARIAN

Indulge in a Vegetarian's Dream at a Steak and Seafood Restaurant, 16

Brake for Lunch at the Original Whistle Stop Café, 17

Red Light Means Go to Chez Lulu, 8

Carve Steaks That Hang off the Plate at Lloyd's Restaurant, 14

Comfort Food Found a New Comfort Zone at Johnny's Restaurant, 19

Soar with Soul Food from the Heart at Eagle's Restaurant, 15

Heat Up at One of the Hottest Restaurants, Hot and Hot Fish Club, 4

Pass the James Beard Awards at Highlands Bar and Grill, 2

You'll Be Over the Moon at the Bright Star, 10

Join a Family Affair at Gianmarco's, 11

• •

FOR THE GULF SEAFOOD LOVER

Pass the James Beard Awards at Highlands Bar and Grill, 2

Heat Up at One of the Hottest Restaurants, Hot and Hot Fish Club, 4

Get a Taste of the Gulf at the Fish Market, 7

You'll Be Over the Moon at the Bright Star, 10

Indulge in a Vegetarian's Dream at a Steak and Seafood Restaurant, 16

Coddle Your Egg at Satterfield's, 9

Make It Automatic for Seafood, 6

Join a Family Affair at Gianmarco's, 11

FOR COCKTAILS

Periodically, You Need a Drink at the Collins Bar, 37

Blast Off to Saturn—Out of This World, 41

Steel Away to Iron City, 43

Pass the James Beard Awards at Highlands Bar and Grill, 2

Unfold a Jazzed-Up Paper Doll, 38

Feel Foxy at the Fennec, 47

Bow Before the Queen, 39

Park Yourself in the Garage for a Great Time, 42

Find the Best Music and Dancing, Bar None, 50

• •

MUSEUM LOVER

Picture Centuries of Beauty at the Birmingham Museum of Art, 92

Honor the Greats at the Negro Southern League Museum, 70

Trace the Road to Freedom on the Civil Rights Trail, 94

Feel Young Again at the Samuel Ullman Museum, 98

Get Your Motor Running at Barber Motorsports, 65

Accelerate to Talladega Superspeedway, 64

Have a Blast at Sloss Furnaces, 96

Enter Birmingham's Antebellum Past at Arlington, 89

Take Off at the Southern Museum of Flight, 97

Vulcan, the God of the Forge, Watches over Us, 86

No Tuxedo Required at the Alabama Jazz Hall of Fame, 99

Walk Where Legends Live On, 68

FREE ENTERTAINMENT

Picture Centuries of Beauty at the Birmingham Museum of Art, 92

Have a Blooming Good Time at the Birmingham Botanical Gardens, 81

Spring for Snowflakes in Aldridge Gardens, 78

Follow the Iron Road at Red Mountain Park, 79

Trace the Road to Freedom on the Civil Rights Trail, 94

Take the Dr. Pepper Cure, 117

Get Rolling at Railroad Park, 76

Learn a Boulder Way to Live at Moss Rock Preserve, 80

Trunks Are Up at Avondale Park, 77

DOWNTOWN

Bow Before the Queen, 39

Periodically, You Need a Drink at the Collins Bar, 37

Get Rolling at Railroad Park, 76

Play Ball at Regions Field/Classic at Rickwood, 66

Picture Centuries of Beauty at the Birmingham Museum of Art, 92

Experiment at the McWane Science Center, 87

Make Moorish Fun at the Alabama Theater, 52

Return to the Golden Era at the Lyric Theater, 53

Pit Masters Rule in Alabama Barbecue, 28

Take the Brews Cruise, It's Pretty Crafty, 48

Trace the Road to Freedom on the Civil Rights Trail, 94

Encounter Reel Fun at the Sidewalk Film Fest, 54

Make the Magic City Art Connection, Bridging People to Art, 58

Feel Foxy at the Fennec, 47

ONLY IN BIRMINGHAM

Vulcan, the God of the Forge, Watches over Us, 86

Dig the Time before Dinosaurs Roamed, 88

Tune to Colonial with the National Sacred Harp Singing Convention, 55

Encounter Reel Fun at the Sidewalk Film Fest, 54

Going to the Dogs on Do Dah Day, 57

Make the Magic City Art Connection, Bridging People to Art, 58

Canoe the Cahaba, Swim in a Swimming Hole, 74

Shhhh . . . Find the Secret Stages, 59

Have a Blast at Sloss Furnaces, 96

Prepare for a Sensory Overload at Joe Minter's Yard, 93

Take Off at the Southern Museum of Flight, 97

Picture Centuries of Beauty at the Birmingham Museum of Art, 92

Trace the Road to Freedom on the Civil Rights Trail, 94

Feast on Football, Food, and Fun at the Magic City Classic, 71

Embrace Your Inner Tacky at the Wacky Tacky Light Tours, 61

FAMILY FUN

Act Right for the Children, 103

Drink in an Opera Shot, 35

Have a Blooming Good Time at the Birmingham Botanical Gardens, 81

Dig the Time before Dinosaurs Roamed, 88

Vulcan, the God of the Forge, Watches over Us, 86

Spring for Snowflakes in Aldridge Gardens, 78

Get Rolling at Railroad Park, 76

Trunks Are Up at Avondale Park, 77

Set Your Compass for Oak Mountain State Park, 73

Play Ball at Regions Field/Classic at Rickwood, 66

Follow the Iron Road at Red Mountain Park, 79

Learn a Boulder Way to Live at Moss Rock Preserve, 80

Horn In on a Roaring Good Time at the Birmingham Zoo, 82

Experiment at the McWane Science Center, 87

Make Moorish Fun at the Alabama Theater, 52

Take Off at the Southern Museum of Flight, 97

Going to the Dogs on Do Dah Day, 57

Party with Gusto at the Greek Festival, 60

Pop Goes the Summer Heat with Popsicles and Ice Cream, 21

Pit Masters Rule in Alabama Barbecue, 28

A Lot of Shaking Going On at Green Valley Drugs, 20

Canoe the Cahaba, Swim in a Swimming Hole, 74

Get Dolled Up for Barbie's Dreamhouse, 116

Act Right for the Children, 103

Embrace Your Inner Tacky at the Wacky Tacky Light Tours, 61

CHEAP EATS

Milo's Is Known for Its Hamburger, Famous for Its Tea, 24

Pit Masters Rule in Alabama Barbecue, 28

Black-Eyed Peas and Turnip Greens Make Pizza Southern Style, 26

Soar Soul Food from the Heart at Eagle's Restaurant, 15

Yo' Mama Knows Her Fried Chicken . . . 13

Indulge in a Vegetarian's Dream at a Steak and Seafood Restaurant, 16

A Lot of Shaking Going On at Green Valley Drugs, 20

You Won't Find Your Average Junkyard Dog at Gus's, 22

• •

DATE NIGHT

Ride the Blimp to Roots and Revelry, 12

Make It Automatic for Seafood, 6

Coddle Your Egg at Satterfield's, 9

Red Light Means Go to Chez Lulu, 8

Join a Family Affair at Gianmarco's, 11

Pass the James Beard Awards at Highlands Bar and Grill, 2

Have a Blooming Good Time at the Birmingham Botanical Gardens, 81

Soar as High Culture Dances, Sings, and Plays, 34

Canoe the Cahaba, Swim in a Swimming Hole, 74

Get Rolling at Railroad Park, 76

Return to the Golden Era at the Lyric Theater, 53

LOL in Real Time at the Comedy Club, 36

Blast Off to Saturn—Out of This World, 41

Put a Song in Your Heart at Red Mountain Theatre, 102

Make Moorish Fun at the Alabama Theater, 52

Encounter Reel Fun at the Sidewalk Film Fest, 54

Vulcan, the God of the Forge, Watches over Us, 86

Find the Best Music and Dancing, Bar None, 50

Bow Before the Queen, 39

Rise as the Moon Shines on the Sleeping Lady, 40

At 2 a.m., Where Do You Go? To the Nick, 51

Museum-quality fossils found on a fossil hunt
led by Fresh Air Family

Photo courtesy of Mark Peavy

INDEX

Alabama Antique Trail, 120

Alabama Booksmith, 118

Alabama Sports Hall of Fame, 68

Alabama Symphony Orchestra, 34

Alabama Theater, 52

Aldridge Gardens, 78

Arlington Antebellum Home & Gardens, 89

art, 37, 38, 58, 77, 78, 92, 93, 100, 102, 117

Avondale Brewing Company, 48–49

Avondale Park, 77, 82

Back Forty Beer Company, 48–49

ballet, 34, 52

Bar 31, 50

barbecue, 14, 28–31

Barber Motorsports, 65

baseball, 70

basic., 110

Bessemer, 10, 23, 28, 31

Bethel Baptist Church, 95

Big Spoon Creamery, 21

Birmingham Botanical Gardens, 81

Birmingham Children's Theater, 103

Birmingham Museum of Art, 92

• •

Bob Sykes Bar-B-Q, 28, 31

books, 118–119, 124

Bridge + Root, 112

Bright Star, 10

Cahaba Brewing Company, 48–49

Cahaba River, 37

Cahaba River Society, 75

canoeing, 73, 74–75

Chez Lulu, 8

Civil Rights Institute, 94–95

Civil Rights Trail, 94–95

cocktails, 2, 4, 6, 12, 37, 38, 39, 40, 45, 47, 107

Collins Bar, 37

Comedy Club, 36

Davenport's Pizza Palace, 26–27

Demetri's BBQ, 28, 31

Do Dah Day, 57

Dog Park, 79

dolls, 93, 116

Downtown, 13, 28, 35, 58, 59, 66, 67, 76, 86, 87, 107, 122

Eagle's Restaurant, 15

Elyton Hotel, 40

fashion, 108, 109, 110, 111, 112, 114

Fennec, 47

Ferus Artisan Ales, 49

Fish Market Restaurant, 7

• •

Garage, 42

gardens, 4, 78, 81, 89, 115

Ghost Train Brewing Company, 48–49

Gianmarco's, 11

Golden Rule Bar-B-Q and Grill, 28, 30

golf, 68, 72, 73

Good People Brewing Company, 49

Greek Festival, 60

Green Valley Drugs, 20

Gus's Hot Dogs, 22

Highlands Bar and Grill, 2

hockey, 67

Homewood, 11, 18, 19, 21, 23, 25, 30–31, 106, 114, 116, 118–119

Hoover, 14, 20–21, 23, 27, 30, 36, 72, 78, 80, 119

Hot and Hot Fish Club, 4–5

hot dogs, 22

ice cream, 9, 21, 117

Iron City, 43

Irondale Café, 17

jazz, 38, 41, 48, 77, 99

jewelry, 108, 120, 122

Jim 'N Nick's Bar-B-Q, 28, 30

Jim Reed Books, 124

Johnny's Restaurant, 19

LeNell's Beverage Boutique, 107

Lloyd's Restaurant, 14

Lyric Theater, 53

Magic City Art Connection, 58

Magic City Classic, 71

Marble Ring, 45

Mary Charles Doll House, 116

McWane Science Center, 87, 88

meat and threes, 10, 16, 19, 26

men's clothing, 112

Milo's Hamburgers, 24–25

Minter, Joe 84, 93

Miss Myra's Pit Bar-B-Q, 31

Moon Shine, 40

Moss Rock Preserve, 80

motorcycles, 65

mountain Biking, 73

Mountain Brook, 27, 109, 119, 122

Museum of Flight, 97

museums, 65, 68, 70, 86, 92, 97, 98, 99, 116, 124

Negro Southern League Museum, 70

Nick, the, 51

Niki's West Steak and Seafood Restaurant, 16

Oak Hill Cemetery, 91

Oak Mountain State Park, 73

opera, 8, 34, 35, 52

orienteering, 73

• •

Queen's Park Cocktail Bar, 39

Quest, the, 46

Paper Doll Bar, 38

Peanut Depot, 123

Pepper Place Market, 117

pizza, 8, 26–27

popsicles, 21

Post Office Pies, 26

racing, 65, 73

Railroad Park, 76

Red Mountain Park, 79

Regions Field, 66

Rib-It-Up, 28, 31

Rickwood Field, 66

Robert Trent Jones Golf Courses, 72

Sacred Harp Singing, 55

Satterfield's Restaurant, 9

Saturn, 41

Saw's BBQ, 28, 30

Secret Stages Music Discovery Festival, 59

Sidewalk Film Festival, 54

Slice Pizza & Brew, 27

Sloss Furnaces, 96

Sneaky Pete's, 22–23

soccer, 67

sports, 68, 73, 64, 65, 67

• •

Steel City Pops, 21

swimming, 16, 73, 74

Talladega Superspeedway, 64

theater, 52, 53, 54, 77, 99, 100, 101, 102, 103

Tortugas Homemade Pizza, 26–27

Trim Tab Brewing Company, 49

Trussville, 23, 25, 30, 48, 49, 119, 121

Turkey Creek Nature Preserve, 74–75

Urban Pops, 21

Vestavia Hills, 9, 25, 31

Veterans Day, 56

Vulcan, 86

Wacky Tacky Light Tour, 61

zoo, 77, 82